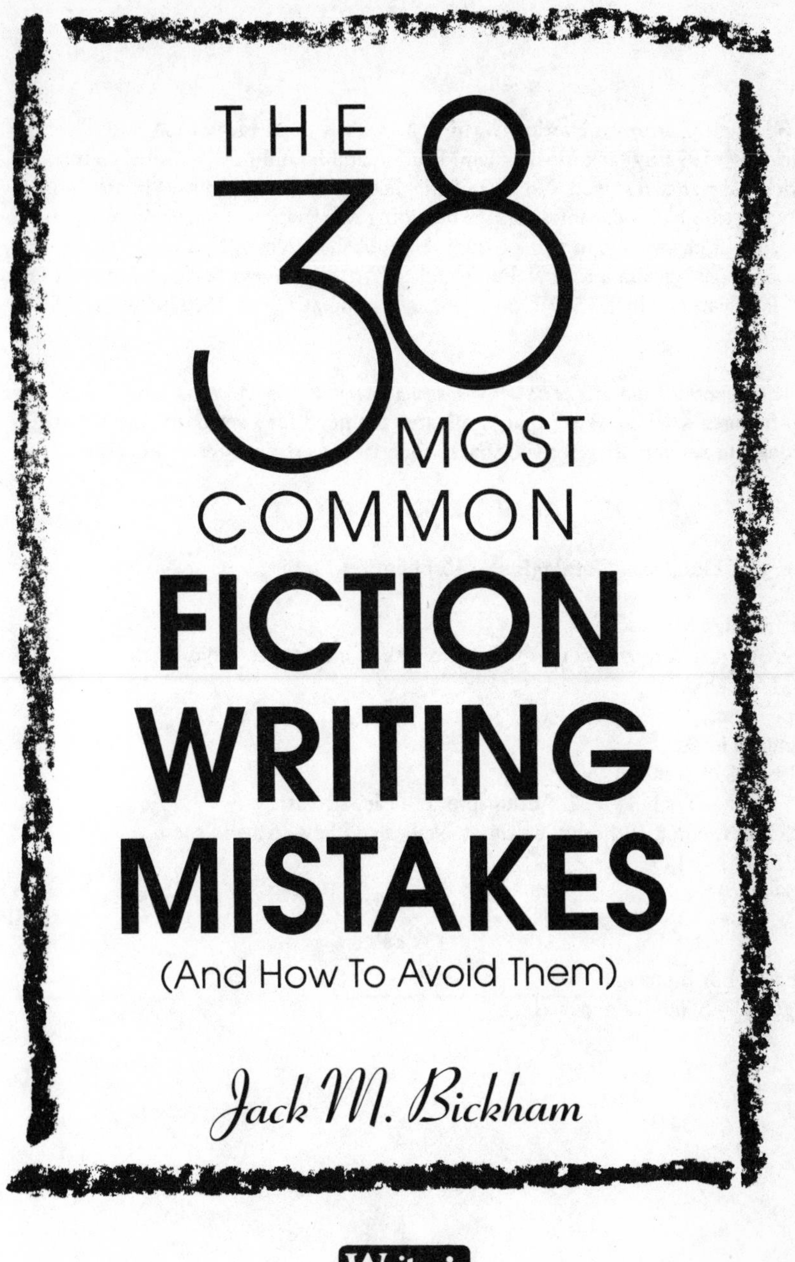

THE 38 MOST COMMON FICTION WRITING MISTAKES

(And How To Avoid Them)

Jack M. Bickham

Cincinnati, Ohio

 Published by Writer's Digest Books, an imprint of F&W Publications, Inc., 1507 Dana Avenue, Cincinnati, Ohio 45207; (800)289-0963. First edition.

This hardcover edition of *The 38 Most Common Fiction Writing Mistakes (and How to Avoid Them)* features a "self-jacket" that eliminates the need for a separate dust jacket. It provides sturdy protection for your book while it saves paper, trees and energy.

96 95 94 93 92 5 4 3 2 1

Library of Congress Cataloging in Publication Data

Bickham, Jack M.
The 38 most common fiction writing mistakes and how to avoid them / Jack M. Bickham.
p. cm.
Includes index.
ISBN 0-89879-503-6 (hrdcvr)
1. Fiction—Technique. 2. Authorship. I. Title. II. Title: The 38 most common fiction writing mistakes and how to avoid them.
PN3355.B47 1992
808.3—dc20 91-32293
CIP

Edited by Bill Brohaugh
Designed by Sandy Conopeotis

About the Author

JACK M. BICKHAM IS THE AUTHOR OF MORE THAN SIXTY-FIVE PUBLISHED NOVELS and numerous publications on the craft of fiction. A David Ross Boyd Professor at the University of Oklahoma (the institution's highest honor for teaching), he left the classroom in 1991 in order to catch up on several writing projects and "look around for a new teaching environment." He says he hopes to return to teaching soon.

Forward

THE PRELIMINARY SECTION OF A BOOK IS OFTEN LABELED A "FOREWORD." BUT in a book involving fiction technique, the word ought to be "Forward."

Why? . . . To emphasize two vital points: *All good fiction moves forward; all good fiction writers look ahead.*

In more than twenty years of teaching courses in professional writing at the University of Oklahoma, I think I've encountered almost every difficulty an aspiring writer might face. (Once, I had a young male student who was both deaf and blind. He required a companion in the classroom to tap her fingers against his hand during my lectures to spell out my words.) But by far the most common—and crippling—problem for students over the years was the tendency to write static copy that didn't have forward movement. And the second most common problem was the habit of looking backwards—at past mistakes and disappointments, or at worries about the part of the story already written—rather than *ahead*, where all the potential . . . all the challenge . . . all the excitement and triumph . . . have to be.

So, despite the fact that I've chosen to write this book from what seems a negative stance, telling you what you shouldn't do, please don't fall into the trap of thinking negatively, or backwards, about your writing. My hope is that by seeing a common error stated boldly in the section heading, you will look harder at your own copy to see if you might be committing the same mistake. But my message is positive—*always.* In every section you'll find a common mistake described, but you'll also find how to avoid that error, or build in a strength as a replacement for a previous weakness.

Nothing can erode your powers more than a negative attitude.

Nothing can cripple your fiction more than looking at it backwards, as a static artifact or "done deal" rather than a living, forward-moving, dynamic series of inventions.

So you'll be reading a lot of "don't" statements in the following pages. But that's partly just to get your attention. Remember, behind every negative is a positive.

Just as behind every rejection there's a triumphant sale—if you'll just persevere.

So let's move on, now . . . *forward.*

—J.M.B.

Table of Contents

1

Don't Make Excuses

WRITERS ARE A FAVORITE SUBJECT FOR CARTOONISTS, FROM CHARLES SCHULZ of *Peanuts* fame to those who contribute to *The New Yorker*. (You can't blame them for picking on writers; we *are* sort of weird.) Over the years I've haphazardly collected such cartoons, and some of my favorites are taped to the door of my office.

One of these shows a nonwriter telling a weary novelist at an autograph party, "Gosh! I know I could write a novel too, but I've just never found the time!"

Another, in two panels, is titled, "Writer's Block." The first panel shows the writer standing idle in his writing room; that panel is captioned "Temporary." In the second panel, the erstwhile writer is standing in the doorway of his fish store; that panel is captioned "Permanent."

A third cartoon shows a writer at his typewriter, telling his wife, "I just can't start until inspiration strikes." Subsequent panels show him in the same position—nothing done—and getting older . . . and older . . . and older.

I don't know how funny these cartoons *really* are, but I like them because they illustrate the primary habit that separates the writers from the pretenders. The world is brimming over with people good enough to make a living as writers. Thank goodness—for those of us who are working, and don't need any more competition—most such talented people spend their creative energies making excuses, and never quite get around to the job at hand.

If you are serious about the craft of fiction, you must never make excuses for yourself. You simply cannot allow yourself to:

- Say you're too tired.
- Postpone work until "later."
- Fail to work because you're too busy right now.
- Wait for inspiration.
- Plan to get right at it "tomorrow."
- Give up because (editors) (agents) (readers) (critics) are unfair. (Fill in as many as you want.)

- Tell yourself you're too old (or too young) to start.
- Blame others in your family for your lack of free time.
- Say your job is too demanding to allow you any other activity.
- Tell yourself that your story idea isn't good enough.

Or any of a host of other excuses you may dream up for yourself.

No. Let's get this straight right away: Writers write; everyone else makes excuses.

Nothing short of a genuine tragedy in your life should be allowed to intrude into your regular work as a writer of fiction. Do you really think successful writers have unlimited time, face no other demands on them, are always peppy and eager to face the keyboard? Of course not! Writing can be tremendous fun, and wonderfully rewarding. But writing is hard work.

Let me repeat.

Writing is hard work.

Nobody really enjoys hard work day after day, week after week. Everybody wants sometimes to get away and play, or just be lazy. When a project such as a novel is going badly, the writer never wants to face her day's stint at the keyboard. At such times, excuses come easily. But the professional simply does not let herself off so easily. All the excuses, all the complaints, all the alternatives to work, must be fought through; the real writer *will work*. And regularly.

Consider: If you write only one page a day, by the end of one year you will have a 365-page novel. Take the next year to rewrite it at the same pace, and you will have a finished novel to show to an agent or editor, which is about the same output that many best-selling novelists have.

If, on the other hand, you make excuses for yourself half the time, then at best it will take you *four* years to have a book ready. That's too long.

And if you make excuses for yourself three-fourths of the time, you will probably lose so much momentum that you'll never finish your project at all.

Consistent, persistent, even dogged work, day in and day out, is the professional's way. And if at the end of a long period of dogged work, your story happens to be rejected, you can't afford to use the rejection as an excuse to quit producing, either. All writers produce some unsalable work. All writers get discouraged, tired and worn down. The good ones don't make excuses. They keep going.

Let me suggest a simple device that may help you avoid the trap of falling into excuse-making. Go find a cheap calendar, the type that has a small open block for each day of the month. At the end of each day, write down in the day's block two things: 1. the number of hours you spent at the typewriter or word processor, working on your fiction project; and 2. how many pages you produced (rough draft or finished, makes no difference) in that working day.

For those days when you don't have anything in terms of work to report, type one double-spaced page of excuses, date it carefully, and file it in a special place. Make sure your excuses fill at least one page, about 250 words. You must do this without fail every time you don't work.

I guarantee you one thing: If you follow this system religiously, you'll soon get so sick of writing down your flimsy excuses that you'll either start investing your time in writing that's more creative, or you'll quit.

In either case you'll have stopped kidding yourself.

No excuse is good enough. Think back to that young man I mentioned in the "Forward." Blind and deaf, *yet he wrote everyday*! You can do no less if you really want to succeed.

2

Don't Consider Yourself Too Smart

IT'S POSSIBLE TO SABOTAGE YOUR FICTION BY BEING TOO SMART FOR YOUR own good—by being a smart aleck. Even before you begin writing your next story, you should examine your attitudes toward yourself, your readers, your own work and contemporary fiction. It could be that these attitudes are damaging your work without your realizing it.

Ask yourself:

- Do you consider yourself more intelligent than most of the stories and novels you read?
- Do you believe contemporary fiction is sort of beneath you in terms of intellectual attainment?
- Do you figure your readers—when you get them—will be dumb compared to you?
- Do you revel in Proust, adore T.S. Eliot, think there has never been a really great American novelist, and sneer at everything in the popular magazines and the best-sellers lists?

If so, I congratulate you on your self-satisfaction, but warn you that such smug condescension will be the death of you as a writer; at best you'll one day publish obscure little short stories in giveaway magazines for other small-college English teachers like yourself; at worst, on your death bed, you'll whisper to your sister the location of your hidden treasure trove of unpublished fiction, and breathe your last in the vain hope that future generations will revere you like they now do Emily Dickinson.

Wouldn't it be a lot better not to consider yourself so smart? To try to figure out what contemporary readers like—then to work to give them the best stories of that type they ever read?

Condescension is a terrible thing. Readers sense it and are turned off by it. The good writer writes humbly, never in a condescending manner, as if to lesser mortals. As the sign said on many a newsroom wall in the olden days, "Don't write down to your readers; the ones dumber than you can't read."

And in terms of fiction, that statement is absolutely true, because fiction does not come from the head; it comes from the heart. The job of the fiction writer is to plumb the depths of human emotions, and then to portray them . . . re-create them . . . stir them. Bigness of heart—compassion—is far more important than bigness of IQ.

If you consider the public a great unwashed that's somehow beneath you, then, I beg you to work on changing your attitudes. You can't write down to your readers. They will catch your insincerity in an instant and hate you for it.

To put all this another way, consider this:

If you're extremely smart, you're lucky. But if you *are* that intelligent, one of your hardest jobs may be to keep a snobbish attitude out of your work. And you don't have to be that smart to write wonderful fiction . . . if you're sensitive and caring enough.

You might even consider putting the following reminders on the bulletin board in your writing room:

NEVER WRITE DOWN TO YOUR READERS.

DON'T ASSUME YOUR READER IS DUMBER THAN YOU.

NEVER—EVER—SNEER AT PUBLISHED WORK.

THINK YOU'RE TOO SMART TO SELL? BALONEY!

COME DOWN TO EARTH! THAT'S WHERE THE READERS ARE.

3

Don't Show Off When You Write

IF YOU HAVE A SPECIAL AREA OF EXPERTISE—IF YOU'RE A NURSE, FOR EXAMPLE, or a lawyer—your specialized knowledge may be a gold mine you can use as background for your stories. Fiction readers love learning about new things as they read a good story.

If you have a rich and extensive vocabulary, that may also prove to be a useful tool. Or if you happen to be a widely read person, or more cultured and schooled in the arts than the average citizen, this too may help you when you write your fiction.

But just as a little knowledge can be a dangerous thing, too much erudition may be fatal to your fiction if you succumb to the temptation to show it off.

Good fiction writers never show off: dump in abstruse knowledge for its own sake, or purposely use big words when simpler ones would do. They constantly seek ways to work in necessary background information in as unobtrusive a way as possible, and they remember that readers get irritated quickly if a writer's style sends them to the dictionary once or twice every paragraph.

You must remember that readers do not read your story to hear how smart you are, or how complicated you can make your sentences. If you insist on showing off in your copy, readers will flee in droves. It's possible to put even very complex ideas in relatively simple language, and it's equally possible to tell your readers a great deal of fascinating information without making it sound like a self-serving show-off act.

Here's an example of the kind of thing you must *not* do:

> In an obscurantist deluge of extraneous verbiage as an outgrowth of an apparent excessive effort to manifest extraordinary intellectual attainment, the aforesaid man impacted adversely on the totality of his audience in a veritable paradigm of irrelevance.

What the writer was trying to say was:

> The man tried to impress people by talking too much, but nobody liked it.

You might want to examine yourself—and your copy—for smart-alecky stuff like this. You might also comb your copy for specialized terminology that might be written more simply and for information you've put in the story just to show how much you know, rather than because it really contributes to the story.

For nobody likes a smart aleck, and fiction readers can sniff one out a mile away.

4

Don't Expect Miracles

A DOCTOR SPENDS FIVE TO TEN YEARS LEARNING HOW TO BE A DOCTOR. WHY, then, do people think they can learn how to be a professional writer of fiction in a week or a month—or even a year?

The writing of fiction is very deceptive. Like riding a bicycle, it looks easy until you try it. But whereas the bicycle gives you quick and painful proof that riding it isn't quite as easy as it appeared, writing is more subtle; your very first story may look good to you—even though it's almost certainly unpublishable on later reflection.

You came to this book because writing interests you, and you're probably doing some of it. To the task you brought some language skills and a desire to tell stories. Your language skills may be quite good. (I hope so.) You may have wonderful ideas for stories, and you type well, etc., etc.

Does any of this mean you know how to write fiction? Unfortunately, no. The writing of fiction—except in the case of that very rare genius—is a difficult job. It involves the interactive working of dozens of specific, hard-won techniques. It may become an art, but only by first being consummate craft.

Yes, if you have a modicum of talent, you can learn how to do it. But it may take you years.

But, why should that be such bad news? If the task were easy, everybody in the world would be a writer, and your achievement would mean little. Setting out on a difficult course is exciting, and the conclusion can be the triumph of a lifetime.

You may find that it takes many manuscripts . . . and a lot of time . . . to learn the ins and outs of the techniques involved in handling viewpoint, or writing developed scenes, or the like. But as you learn each bit of the craft, paying for your knowledge in hard work and the passage of time, I guarantee that you'll grow more excited about the pursuit . . . more awed by the beauty and logic of how fiction works.

It's worth the time. Expect no overnight miracles, but have faith. If you persevere, the chances are very good that you will achieve some success.

Conversely, if you get disgusted or discouraged, expecting overnight fame and fortune, you're certain to fail. Absolutely.

Write in your journal, or in some other permanent record, your goal as a writer five years from today. Assuming (as is true) that a writing career proceeds by small steps forward—write where you hope ideally to be as a writer four years from now. And in three years. And in two. And by next year this time.

Put that list of hopes aside somewhere safe. Get to work. Be patient, but press yourself to work hard. Make notes of your insights and learned skills as you come upon them. Then, a year from now, compare where you were (now) with where you will be by that time. You'll be surprised and pleased.

Maybe you won't be a selling writer of fiction yet. But you'll be a lot closer and able to see your own progress.

5

Don't Warm Up Your Engines

OFTEN, WHEN I START TO READ A STORY WRITTEN BY AN INEXPERIENCED writer, I am reminded of those cold winter mornings long ago in Ohio when I sat miserably beside my father in the old Buick, in the dark garage, waiting for the engine to warm up before driving away from home.

In those days it was considered good form to warm your engine before driving the car. Multiviscosity engine oil was far in the future, and the theory was that the motor should idle a while under no strain while the heat of ignition warmed the oil so it could circulate more freely, providing better lubrication.

Those days are long gone. But, amazingly, fiction writers still do the same kind of unnecessary and wasteful thing in starting their stories.

"Why," I may ask them, "have you started your story with this long, static description of a town (or a house, or a street, or a country scene)?"

"Well," the beginning writer will reply, puzzled, "I need to set up where the story is going to take place."

Or I may be forced to ask, "Why have you started this story by giving me background information about things that happened months (or even years) ago?"

"Well," the poor neophyte will say, "I wanted the reader to know all that before starting the story."

Such static or backward-looking approaches to fiction are probably lethal in a novel, and are certainly fatal in a modern short story. Readers today—and that of course includes editors who will buy or reject your work—are more impatient than ever before. They will not abide a story that begins with the author warming up his engines. If a setting needs to be described, it can be described later, after you have gotten the story started. If background must be given the reader, it can be given later, *after* you have intrigued him with *the present action of the story*.

I've had the horrific experience of standing in the doorway of a room at a magazine publishing house where first readers go through freelance submissions, deciding whether the stories should be passed on to an editor for further consideration, or sent back as a rejection at once. Sometimes a reader would slit the end of a manila envelope and pull the manuscript only halfway out of the envelope, scanning the first paragraph or two of the yarn. Sometimes—*on the basis of this glance alone*—the story was either passed on to an editor for consideration, or tossed into the reject pile.

Do you think that you're really going to get past that first reader with an unmoving description of a house or a street? Do you imagine that that reader, going through hundreds of manuscripts every day, is going to pass on your story if it begins with stuff that happened twenty years ago?

The chances are very, very slim.

Moral: Don't warm up your engines. *Start the story with the first sentence!*

How do you do that? By recognizing three facts:

1. Any time you stop to describe something, you have *stopped.* Asking a reader to jump eagerly into a story that starts without motion is like asking a cyclist to ride a bike with no wheels—he pedals and pedals but doesn't get anywhere. Description is vital in fiction, but at the outset of the story it's deadly.

2. Fiction looks forward, not backward. When you start a story with background information, you point the reader in the wrong direction, and put her off. If she had wanted old news, she would have read yesterday's newspaper.

3. Good fiction starts with—and deals with—someone's response to threat.

Let's look a bit further at this No. 3, because it tells us how our stories should start.

As human beings, it's in our nature to be fascinated by threat. Start your story with a mountain climber hanging from a cliff by his fingernails, and I guarantee that the reader will read a bit further to see what happens next. Start your story with a child frightened because she has to perform a piano solo before a large recital audience—and feeling threatened, of course—and your reader will immediately become interested in her plight.

It stands to reason, then, that you should not warm up your engines at the outset. You should start the action. What kind of action? *Threat*—and a response to it.

Every good story starts at a moment of threat.

Does this mean you are doomed to spend your writing career looking for new and dire physical threats? I don't think so, although some fine writers have thrived by writing fiction dealing with literal, physical threat and danger. But you don't have to write about physical catastrophe to have fascinating threat in your stories.

Think back a moment over your own life. What were some of the times when you felt most scared, most threatened? Perhaps it was your first day of school. Or at a time when there was a death in the family, or a divorce. Perhaps the first time you had to speak a line in a school play. Or when you tried out for a sports team. Maybe your first date? When you changed schools? When the family moved? When some new people moved in next door to you, and you didn't know if you would like them? When you were engaged or married, or when you started your first real job? When you were fired from a job? Or promoted to a better one?

All stressful events. All threatening, even though many of them were happy occasions. Now, why should that be so? Isn't it strange that happy events would be threatening?

Not at all. Better minds than I have pointed out that we human beings like to feel in harmony with our environment and our situation in life. Each of us carries inside a view of ourselves, our life, and the kind of person we are. When things are going well, we feel in harmony with everything and everyone around us, and we aren't threatened. But enter change—*almost any change*—and our world has been shaken up. We feel uneasy.

Threatened.

Nothing is more threatening than change.

From this, it stands to reason that you will know when and where to start your story—page one, line one—when you identify the moment of change. Because change is where the story starts.

A bus comes to town, and a stranger gets off.

The boss calls an employee: "Please come in here. I have something important to tell you."

A new family moves into the house down the block.

A telegram is delivered to your door.

The seasons change, and you grow restless . . . uneasy.

It is at this moment of crucial change, whatever it may be, that your story starts. Identify the moment of change, and you know when your story must open. To begin in any other way is to invite disaster:

- Open earlier, with background, and it's dull.
- Open by looking somewhere else in the story, and it's irrelevant.
- Open long after the change, and it's confusing.

Begin your story now. Move it forward now. All that background is an author concern. *Readers don't care*. They don't want it. The reader's concern is with change . . . threat . . . how a character will respond *now*.

"But I really like that stuff about Grandpaw and Grandmaw, and how things were in 1931!" I hear you protest. "I want to put that stuff in!"

Not in this story, you can't—not if this story is set in present times. Maybe you can work a little of it into the story later, but starting with it will kill you. (If worse comes to worst, you can write some other story about the 1930s, where the old stuff can become present-day stuff in terms of the story's assumptions.)

Remember what the reader wants. Don't try to inflict *your* author concerns on her. You must give her what she wants at the start, or she'll never read any further.

And what she wants—what will hook her into reading on—is threat.

The most common variety of which is change.

Test yourself on this. In your journal or notebook, make a list of ten times in your life when you felt the most scared or worried.

My list might include my first day at college, the day I entered active duty with the air force, my first formal speech before a large audience, and my first solo in a small plane. Your list might be quite different. But our lists, I'll bet, will have one thing in common. Both will represent moments of change.

Having realized this, you might want to make a second list, this one of ten changes that you think might make good opening threats in stories. It's perfectly all right to build upon some of your own real-life experiences here. It's equally okay to make up threatening changes.

In either case, I suggest that you keep this list, and the next time you catch yourself sensing that the opening of your current fiction project is bogging down or going too slowly, compare your problem opening with your list of ideas in terms of depth and seriousness of the change you're dealing with. Maybe you'll find that you've backslid into warming up your story engines instead of starting with that crucial moment of change that really gets the yarn under way.

6

Don't Describe Sunsets

READERS NEED DESCRIPTION IN THE STORIES THEY READ TO VISUALIZE SETtings and people—really "get into" the action. But sometimes writers get carried away and go too far in trying to provide such descriptions; they stop too often to describe such things as sunsets, thinking that pretty prose is an end in itself—and forgetting that when they stop to describe something at length, the story movement also stops.

A friend of mine, the late Clifton Adams, was an enormously gifted writer of western fiction, short stories and novels. In one of his prizewinning western novels, he devoted several pages to describing a sunset. It was an amazing departure from established norms in professional fiction.

Yet in this isolated circumstance it worked. Adams had set up the story situation in a way that told the reader of a dire threat: as soon as total darkness fell, a band of desperadoes planned to attack the hero's lonely trail camp and do him in. For this reason, every word of the sunset description was relevant—and painfully suspenseful.

Only in such a special situation can you devote great space to description, no matter how poetic it may seem to you. One of the standing jokes among writers and publishers is about the amateur writer who devotes precious space to describing a sunrise or sunset. All you have to do, in some publishing circles, is mention something like "the rosy fingers of dawn" and you get smiles all around. Such descriptions usually are a hallmark of poor fiction writing.

If you've been reading this book straight through from the front, you already see why this is so. Fiction is *movement*. Description is static. Trying to put in a lengthy description of a setting or person in fiction is a little like the dilemma facing physicists when they try to describe the nature of the electron. As one distinguished scientist once put it, "You can describe what an electron is at a given moment, but if you do, you don't know exactly where it is; or you can try to describe where it is, but then you can't say exactly what it is."

Part of what he was saying, I think, was simply this: to describe something in detail, you have to stop the action. But without the action, the description has no meaning.

Therefore, whenever you try to inflict on your readers a detailed description, your story stops. And readers are interested in the story—the movement—not your fine prose.

Does this mean you should have no description in your story? Of course not. Description must be worked in carefully, in bits and pieces, to keep your reader seeing, hearing, and feeling your story world. But please note the language here: it must be *worked in, a bit at a time*, not shoveled in by the page.

I am certainly not the first person to warn about "poetic" descriptions and how they stop a story. And yet they continue to appear again and again in amateur copy. Such segments prove one of two things: either the writer has no understanding of the basic nature of fiction, or the writer is so in love with her own words that she allows arrogance to overcome wisdom. "Fine writing" almost always slows the story's pace and distracts readers from the story line itself.

And note, please, that description can be something other than writing about a tree or a sunset. Beginning writers sometimes make the mistake of stopping everything while they describe *a character's thoughts or feelings*. This often is every bit as bad as the rosy fingers of dawn.

Of course you should and must look into your character's head and heart. And some of your insight must be given the reader, so she can know about the character, sympathize with the character, identify with the action. But in good fiction—even at novel length—such descriptions of the character's state of mind and emotion are usually relatively brief. The accomplished writer will tell (describe) *a little*, and demonstrate (show in action) *a lot*.

Modern readers want you to move the story, not stand around discussing things.

In this regard, you may want to think about your fiction *delivery systems*. There are different ways to deliver your information to your reader. They have characteristic speeds:

- *Exposition*. This is the slowest of all. It's the straight giving of factual information. Nothing whatsoever is happening. You're giving the reader data—biographical data, forensic data, sociological data, whatever. Some of this has to go in your story, but there's no story movement while you're putting in your encyclopedia info.
- *Description*. Almost as slow. Again, some is necessary. But watch it.
- *Narrative*. Here we have characters onstage in the story "now," and their actions, give-and-take, are presented moment by moment, with no summary and nothing left out. This is like a stage play, and much of your story will be in this form, as we'll discuss in a later section. This kind of storytelling goes very swiftly and provides continuous movement.
- *Dialogue*. Story people talking. Very little action or interior thought.

Like a fast-moving tennis match, back and forth, point and counterpoint. When the story people are under stress and talk in short bursts, this is tremendously fast and forward-moving.

▪ *Dramatic Summary*. The fastest form of all. Here you have dramatic stuff happening, but instead of playing it out moment by moment, as in narrative, you choose to add even more speed by summarizing it. In this mode, a car chase or argument that might require six pages of narrative might be condensed into a single light-speed paragraph.

If your stories seem to be moving too slowly, you might analyze some of your copy, looking at what form of writing you tend to use. It could be that you are describing too many sunsets (in one form or another) and never using any dialogue or dramatic summary. On the other hand, if you sense that your stories whiz along at too breakneck a speed, perhaps you need to change some of that dramatic summary into narrative, or even pause (briefly!) now and then to describe what the setting looks like, or what the character is thinking or feeling.

In this way, you can become more conscious of your tendencies as a fiction writer, and begin to see which tendencies help you, and which tend to hold you back from selling. You can learn better to call your shots in terms of pacing your yarn, selecting the delivery system that's needed for the desired effect, and keeping the yarn moving.

7

Don't Use Real People in Your Story

ONE OF MY NEW WRITING STUDENTS, A GENT WE SHALL CALL WALLY, CAME BY my office the other day with the first pages of a new story. I read the pages and then handed them back to him.

"Wally," I complained as gently as I could, "these characters are really not very interesting."

Wally frowned, not understanding.

I tried again: "Wally, these characters are dull. What they are is flat and insipid. They are pasteboard. They have no life, no color, no vivacity. They need a lot of work."

Wally looked shocked. "How can these characters be *dull*? They're *real people*—every one of them! I took them right out of real life!"

"Oh," I said. "So that's the problem."

"What?" he said.

"You can never use real people in your story."

"Why?"

"For one reason, real people might sue you. But far more to the point in fiction copy, real people—taken straight over and put on the page of a story—are dull."

Wally sat up straighter. "Are you telling me my friends are dull?"

"Of course not!" I told him. "That's not the point. The point is that in fiction real people aren't vivid enough. Good characters have to be constructed, not copied from actuality."

Wally was discouraged. But I tried to explain it to him with something like this:

One of the toughest jobs we ask of our readers is to see characters vividly and sympathize with them. Consider: all your readers have to go by are some symbols printed on a sheet of paper. From these symbols, readers must recognize letters of the alphabet, make the letters into words, derive meaning from the words, link the meanings into sentences. From that point, readers must make an even more amazing leap of faith or intuition of some kind: they must use their own imagination to picture—physically and emotionally—a person inside their own head. And then they must believe this imagined person is somehow real—and even care about him.

Readers need all the help they can get to perform this arduous imaginative-emotional task. They have a lot to see through to get the job done even imperfectly.

To help them, you can't simply transcribe what you see and know about a real person. You have to *construct* something that is far bigger than life, far more *exaggerated*. Then, if you do your job of exaggeration extremely well, your readers will see your gross exaggeration dimly, but well enough to think, "This constructed character looks like a real person to me."

Good fiction characters, in other words, are never, ever real people. Your idea for a character may begin with a real person, but to make him vivid enough for your readers to believe in him, you have to exaggerate tremendously; you have to provide shortcut identifying characteristics that stick out all over him, you have to make him practically a monster—for readers to see even his dimmest outlines.

Thus, even if you start with some real person, you won't end up with him as your character.

For example, if your real person is loyal, you will make your *character* tremendously, almost unbelievably loyal; if he tends to be a bit impatient in real life, your character will fidget, gnash his teeth, drum his fingers, interrupt others, twitch, and practically blow sky high with his outlandishly exaggerated impatience. In addition, you may find that it helps your creation if you take one or two other real-life people and add *their* most exaggerated impatient characteristics.

What you will end up with, if you do well, will be a dimly perceived construct who no longer bears any resemblance to the real person with whom you started. Because good characters are in no way like real people . . . not really.

In addition, to create a fictional character, you will give him some highly recognizable tags that are—again—more exaggerated than anything we'll ever encounter in real life. Thus our impatient character will also be nervous. He'll smoke, a lot. He'll always be lighting a cigarette, asking for a match, putting out a cigarette, puffing smoke. His habit of drumming his fingers on the table will be shown often, as another tag of impatience and nervousness. He'll interrupt people and be rude—push past others to get into the elevator, give snappish answers to questions, honk his horn at the driver in front of him the instant the light turns green, and so on. And all these tags that you devise will be waved often, not just occasionally, as they might appear in real life.

Good fiction characters also tend to be more understandable than real-life people. They do the things they do for motives that make more sense than real-life motives often do. While they're more mercurial and colorful, they're also more goal-motivated. Readers must be able to understand why your character does what he does; they may not agree with his motives, but you have carefully set things up so at least they can see that he's acting as he is *for some good reason.*

In all these ways fiction characters are not just different than life. They're better. Bigger. Brighter. More understandable. Nicer or meaner. Prettier or uglier. And ultimately more fascinating.

I can almost hear your silent protest: "But I want to write realistic fiction." Good. So do I. Yet, to convey an illusion of realism, you as a good fiction writer can never transcribe real people; you must build your characters, taking aspects of real people and exaggerating some angles while suppressing others, adding a bit of Charlie's choleric nature to Archibald's pathos, tossing in some of Andrew's brittle way of talking, salting with your own list of tags that you made up from your imagination, sticking on the motives, plans, hopes and fears that you made up as the author for this character because they're what you as the author need to have in this particular story.

Even the *names* of your characters are constructed. "Brick Bradley" by his very name is a different character from "Percy Flower." "Mother Theresa" can never be the same kind of person as a "Dolores LaRue." Even your character names are constructs, not reality.

And consider *character background.* In real life, a young woman may come out of a poverty-stricken rural background and still somehow become the president of a great university. Except in a long novel, where you might have sufficient space to make it believable, you would have a hard time selling this meshing of background and present reality in fiction. Chances are that in a short story you would make up a far different background for your female university president, perhaps constructing an early life as the favorite or only daughter of a college professor mother and physician father. (In short fiction, characters and their backgrounds are almost always much more consistent than people in real life.)

Motivation? Again, fictional characters are better than life. In real life, people often seem to do things for no reason we can understand. They act on impulses that grow out of things in their personalities that even *they* sometimes don't understand. But in fiction there is considerably less random chance. While good characters are capable of surprising readers—and should sometimes do so for verisimilitude—such characters are always understandable on fairly simple later analysis.

To put this point another way, in real life people often don't make sense. But in fiction, they do.

The author sees to that.

Just as she sees to many other things about her characters, remembering always that fiction people are *not* real people.

It's just one of several ways that fiction surpasses and improves upon life. And that's a good thing, isn't it? After all, if fiction were really just like life, why would we have to have it at all? What need would it meet? Who would care about it?

We spin tales . . . make up story people. None of it is real, and therein lies its beauty. In your stories, as in all the stories ever told, you must hold the magnifying glass up to your people and events for readers to appreciate them at all . . . and thus briefly enter a private world, largely of their own imagining—*made vivid by your crafty help*.

8

Don't Write About Wimps

Fiction writers too often forget that interesting characters are almost always characters who are active—risk-takers—highly motivated toward a goal. Many a story has been wrecked at the outset because the writer chose to write about the wrong kind of person—a character of the type we sometimes call a wimp.

You know what a wimp is.

He's the one who wouldn't fight under any circumstances.

Ask him what he wants, and he just sighs.

Poke him, and he flinches—and retreats.

Confront him with a big problem, and he fumes and fusses and can't make a decision.

Now, in real life there are a lot of wimps. You and I have both been wimpy far more often than we would like to admit. We get confused, we get scared, we get far too ambivalent, and we just sit around and wait to see what might happen next.

To put it another way, in reality—in the real world—much of what happens is accidental. "Isn't life funny!" we exclaim, after fate has taken a hand and something has worked out by itself, seemingly. And so we stagger on, major life changes just sort of happening, and we often don't take the bull by the horns because we can't even figure out where the damned bull is.

That's reality.

But fiction isn't reality; as we said before, it's better.

So, in most effective fiction, accidents don't determine the outcome. And your story people don't sit around passively. (Now and then you'll find a story in which what I've just said is disproven; but I'm talking about *most* successful fiction. Most readers don't want their stories to tell them life is random. They want to hear just the opposite. They want to believe something. What they want to believe is that trying hard can pay off, and that people are in charge of their own fate.)

That's why wimps—spineless drifters who won't or can't rouse themselves to try—usually make terrible fiction characters.

Good fiction characters are fighters. They know what they want, they encounter trouble, and they struggle. They don't give up and they don't retire from the action. They don't wait for fate to settle the issue. In good fiction, *the story people determine the outcome.* Not fate. This is just another of the many ways in which fiction surpasses life and is better than real life.

Look at it this way: A good story is the record of movement. A good story *is* movement. Someone pushes; someone else pushes back. At some level, therefore, a story is the record of a fight.

If you accept this premise, then it's obvious that you can't invest the action and outcome of your story in a wimp. He'll refuse to struggle, won't push back when shoved, and will run and hide at the first opportunity.

"I just can't make anything happen in my story," you'll hear another writer complain. Or, "I've got a good idea, but can't seem to keep it moving." Or, "Something is wrong with my new story; it seems dull, and the characters are lifeless." In all such cases, the real problem is not with plot, but with the kind of central character the writer has chosen to write about. Jerk that wimp out of the story and put in someone who will press ahead like the movie characters that John Wayne used to play, or the ones usually portrayed today by someone like Clint Eastwood. Now something will start happening!

Does this mean that every character has to be as violent and headlong as a Clint Eastwood movie character? By no means. Just because a character is strongly goal-motivated and active doesn't mean he has to be a superhero. A character may be active—refuse to give up or stop trying—yet still be scared or sometimes unsure of himself. In actuality, such a character, who acts despite worry or fear, is stronger than the one who simply plunges onward without doubt or thought.

How do you build a strong character who will act and not be a wimp? In the first place, you determine to do so. You throw away any wrong ideas you may have about the quiet, contemplative, sensitive, thoughtful character, and recognize that it isn't very interesting, watching somebody sit in his easy chair and *ponder things*. Your character has to be a person capable of action, and that's for starters.

Now, having decided that you'll write about someone who is willing to do something rather than sit around and await the workings of fate, you have to nudge him into action. How do you do that? By hitting him with that threatening change we talked about earlier.

At this point, you put yourself in your character's shoes and begin to give him a game plan. This is his response to whatever threatening change now faces him. He does *not* give up or whine; he decides to do something to fix his plight. He sets out with a *goal*. He is committed. Attainment of his goal is essential to his happiness.

All well and good. Having come this far, you have started to build your story as a quest. Virtually all contemporary fiction, at some level, is the record of such a quest. The "Indiana Jones" thrillers worked on the big screen because they were pure quest (in the third such adventure, it was literally a quest for the Holy Grail). Your story may involve a lesser goal, literally speaking, but it can be no less vital to your character.

Something has changed.

Your character is threatened.

He vows to struggle.

He selects a goal and starts taking action toward it.

And you have a story under way.

It sounds simple enough, doesn't it? Then why do so many writers make it so hard?

Why, for example, do they let themselves get so tangled up in background information that the character has to sit around for page after page, while the author does a core dump of old information? Why do they let the character worry and fume for page after page instead of *doing something*? Why do they plunge into Freudian analysis of the poor guy instead of letting him get off the couch and get after it?

Confusion of confusions, all is confusion when you forget, even briefly, and allow your character to act like a wimp. Male or female, young or old, lovelorn or treasure-bound, your central story person has to *act*. And he has to confront at least one other story person who is also decidedly un-wimpy, so there can be a struggle. The minute somebody quits or retires from the action even temporarily, your story dies on the vine.

We're talking here mainly about major characters in your story. But even minor characters may suffer from passivity. You should examine *all* your characters to see if making them stronger-acting might make them also more vivid and interesting. For the wimpy character usually tends to fade into the woodwork and be dull.

Now, this may sound like I'm arguing for only one kind of story, an action/adventure. Nothing could be further from the truth. While a strong, goal-motivated character is easier seen in such a yarn, the effective character in even the quietest modern story will almost always be a person capable of action. In a romance novel, for example, the young woman may seem unwilling to face the man to whom she is attracted and may even deny her own feelings and actively avoid him. But please note that she is taking action, even if it is sometimes negative. In a psychological story about a man assailed by self-doubt and uncertainty, he will realize that he has a problem and see a doctor or take a pill or discuss it with a friend or write a letter or *do something*.

So that—to repeat for emphasis—every story is the record of a quest. An active character worth writing about will form some goal, based on his plight and his motives. He will *work* toward that goal, not sit back passively. And—wonder to behold—his active selection of a goal will be picked up by the reader and used as a basis for suspense.

Any time a character forms a goal-oriented intention in fiction, the reader will turn the goal statement around and make it into a *story question*—

and then begin worrying about it! This is an activity at which the reader is wonderfully adept. You give your un-wimpy character the goal of finding his lost sister, and the reader instantly worries, *Will* he find his lost sister? Or you give your character the specific goal of winning a better job, and your reader immediately worries, *Will* she get the better job?

From this process of reader-translation—character goal to story question—comes reader worry, or to give it another name, suspense.

Let me suggest that you look hard and long at the kind of characters you typically tend to write about. Are any of them wimps? Do they whine or sit around passively or "wait and see"? If so, they may be at the heart of your problems as a writer of fiction.

How do you get them going? First you change your assumptions about what makes a good fiction character. Then you present them with a pressing problem. Then you decide what they are going to do about it—*now*. And finally you keep them moving, continuing to struggle; you never allow them to give up or retire from the story action. They move and they press and they keep on, always questing after their goal, whether it's a date to the high school prom or the Holy Grail.

Same thing, ultimately. Because whatever it is, it's essential to your character's happiness, and *that character will not give up*. He's determined; he's going to try and try again. He's going to fight to maintain control of his life—and determine his own destiny.

I like him, don't you?

I care about him already, don't you?

9

Don't Duck Trouble

IN FICTION, THE BEST TIMES FOR THE WRITER—AND READER—ARE WHEN THE story's main character is in the worst trouble. Let your character relax, feel happy and content, and be worried about nothing, and your story dies. Pour on all sorts of woes so your poor character is thoroughly miserable and in the deepest kind of trouble, and your story perks right up—along with your reader's interest.

The moral: Although most of us do everything we can to avoid trouble in real life, we must do just the opposite as writers of fiction. We must seek out ways to add trouble to our characters' lives, putting just as much pressure on them as we can. For it's from plot trouble that reader interest comes.

There are many kinds of fiction trouble, but the most effective kind is *conflict.*

You know what conflict is. It's active give-and-take, a struggle between story people with opposing goals.

It is *not*, please note, bad luck or adversity. It isn't fate. It's a fight of some kind between people with opposing goals.

Fate, bad luck or whatever you choose to call it may play a part in your fiction too. Adversity—that snowstorm that keeps your character from having an easy drive to the mountain cabin, for example, or the suspicious nature of the townspeople that complicates your detective's investigation—is nice, too. But these problems are blind; they are *forces* of some kind that operate willy-nilly, without much reason—and so are things that your character can't confront and grapple with.

In other words, it's all well and good to have your character leave his house in the morning and slip and fall on a banana peel, thus making him feel bad all day. But such an event comes out of nowhere for no good reason; like real-life events, it makes no sense. It is caused by nothing much and leads to nothing special.

Adversity in all its forms may create some sympathy for your character. But your character can't reasonably try to understand it, plot against it, or even confront it in a dramatic way.

Conflict, on the other hand, is a fight with another person. It's dramatic, onstage now, with the kind of seesaw give-and-take that makes most sporting events—many courtroom trials—exciting stuff. When in conflict, your character knows who the opponent is and has a chance to struggle against him. In conflict, your character has a chance to change the course of events. In taking the challenge and entering the fray, your character proves himself to be worthy as a story hero: he's trying to take charge of his life . . . determine the outcome . . . *win.*

Thus, if you're a wise writer of fiction, you spend a good deal of your plotting hours devising ways to set up more fights. In real life you might walk around the block to avoid meeting Maryanne, the neighbor who always wants to start an argument with you. In your fiction, you may walk your hero a mile just to get him into position so he *can* have a fight with the person who most irritates him.

The calmer and more peaceful your real life, the better, in all likelihood. Your story person's life is just the opposite. You the author must *never* duck trouble—conflict—in the story. You seek it out, because that's where the excitement and involvement—as well as reader sympathy for your character—lie.

Please note that *conflict* does not necessarily mean an actual physical fight, although sometimes it certainly may be exactly that. Conflict may be any of the following examples:

- Two men argue in a board meeting, each intent on convincing the members of the board that he should be named president of the firm.
- A young woman pleads with her father to accept into the family the man she loves.
- Two cars race along a highway, the driver of one intent on forcing the other off the road.
- A detective persistently questions an uncooperative witness, trying to dig out information that would help solve a murder.
- A man maneuvers in a dark alley, trying to slip away from an armed pursuer whose occasional small sounds give away his position.
- Lovers quarrel.
- A man and woman discuss whether to buy a new car. He wants it; she doesn't.
- A woman reporter tries to get information for a story from a derelict on skid row, but he keeps slipping away from the subject, into reminiscences.
- Daniel Boone fights a bear.

Of course you will think of many more examples, once you have it clear in your mind that conflict always means a fight, at some level.

How do you make sure you have a fight and not some form of blind bad luck?

You make sure two characters are involved.

You give them opposing goals.

You put them onstage now.

You make sure both are motivated to struggle *now*.

Virtually all the high points of most stories involve conflict. It's the fuel that makes fiction go. Nothing is more exciting and involving. And—please note—"fiction friction" of this kind is another example of how fiction is better than life.

In life, you might walk out of your house in the morning and get struck by lightning. Blind luck, meaningless, against which you are powerless. Life is like that. *Dumb!* But in fiction the character has the power: he can control his own destiny, or at least thinks he can. He *will* struggle, if he's worth writing about, and will encounter endless fights. The outcome will depend on him—not on blind luck.

A lot better than life sometimes is, right?

Of course.

10

Don't Have Things Happen for No Reason

ONE MORNING NOT LONG AGO, MY STUDENT WALLY CAME BY THE OFFICE with part of another story. Sipping my second cup of coffee, I read what he had brought to me.

"Wally," I said finally, "this story doesn't make sense."

"What do you mean?" Wally asked.

"I mean your characters don't seem to have any background motivation for their story intentions here, they constantly seem to be running into other people and information strictly by coincidence, and they often do or say things for no apparent immediate reason."

Wally looked blank. "That's bad?"

"Wally, it makes your story totally illogical!"

"Wait a minute," Wally protested. "I don't have to be logical. I'm writing *fiction*!"

It's a fairly common misconception, this one of Wally's. Since fiction is make-believe, says this line of reasoning, then the most important thing is to be imaginative and original—and so anyone who tries to argue for logic and credibility in a story must be trying to thwart somebody's artistic genius.

The truth, as you've probably already begun to see, is just the opposite. Because fiction is make-believe, it has to be *more logical* than real life if it is to be believed. In real life, things may occur for no apparent reason. But in fiction you the writer simply cannot ever afford to lose sight of logic and let things happen for no apparent reason.

To make your stories logical, and therefore believable, you work always to make sure there is always a reason for what happens.

For one thing, you always provide characters with the right background—upbringing, experience, information—to motivate them generally in the direction of the action you want to show them taking.

A character, if she is to act with seeming reason, must come from a personal background that qualifies her to accomplish your plot action. You must set things up so that her general background—family, upbringing, education, health, whatever—make it seem reasonable that she would act as you want her to act in the story.

As an extreme example here, let's say you want your character to preach a sermon some Sunday in a Southern Baptist church, citing the life of Christ as the perfect type for all to emulate. Only a slow thinker would fail to put *something* in the story earlier to show how the character was either brought up in a Christian home, or went through a religious conversion to Christianity. Thus the general background must be given, or else the character's actions may seem to come from no logical origin.

Following the same example a step further, remember that the general background may not be enough. Your readers will also want to know the more recent event or events that have given your character the motivation to do what she is doing right now. Thus, in the example cited, you might have the Christian woman's minister husband fall suddenly ill, which prompts her, in desperation, to fill in for him after the congregation has already assembled. Or you might set things up so the sermon is to be some kind of test set up by the church's governing board. Whatever you pick, you will pick something that will explain how and why she got up there in the pulpit now, doing what you the writer want her to do in the way you want her to do it.

(Do you want her to be nervous or calm? Sad or happy? You'll need to provide recent cause for these desired aspects of her performance, too.)

A great many stories tend to be unbelievable because the writer just shoved a character onstage to do something without thinking through how and why the character got there. You must constantly examine your story logic to make sure you have not inadvertently committed the same error.

But problems with logic in your fiction don't end with background motivation. Another kind of error that can destroy the evident logic of a story is the use of excessive luck or coincidence.

In real life, coincidence happens all the time. But in fiction—especially when the coincidence helps the character be at the right place at the right time, or overhear the crucial telephone conversation, or something similar—coincidence is deadly. Your readers will refuse to believe it. And you can't afford to let your readers stop believing.

When the long arm of coincidence helps your character along, it's just good luck. Reading about someone blundering along, getting lucky, is neither very interesting nor very inspiring. A story filled with coincidence tends to make no sense because there is no real reason why things happen—they just happen.

In real life that's good enough. In fiction it isn't.

Now you may see another reason why we advised you not to write about wimps in Chapter Eight. To get a wimp to accomplish anything, you almost have to fall back on incredible coincidence, which erodes reader belief and makes your story an accidental mess.

Your character can't sit home passively and accidentally get a telephone call from friend Max, who then volunteers a crucial clue in the murder mystery. Your character has to think things over and then decide that *he will call people seeking information.* After calling several other people, he comes to Max on his list. He calls Max. Max doesn't want to tell him, but you make your character persist. Finally your character convinces Max to talk, and Max gives him the next clue.

This way, instead of being fat, dumb and happy—and having a stroke of good luck for no reason—your character instead has worked for what he has gotten. And that is satisfying.

First-draft fiction tends to be full of unrealized coincidences. Your character goes to a strange town and "just happens" to meet an old friend on the street. Or she gets to buy a long-coveted new dress because she "just happens" to walk by the store on the one afternoon when it's for sale, and it "just happens" to fit her perfectly, and she "just happens" to get there five minutes before Annabelle, who also wanted the dress.

Readers may not realize why they don't believe your story when you allow this kind of sloppy plot planning to ease the way for you, but they won't like it.

After your first draft, watch with an eagle eye for coincidences, either ones you might have impatiently allowed in the first write-through just to get on with it, or (even worse) those you simply didn't recognize earlier as outlandishly lucky.

How do you fix coincidence? First, you excise it. Second, you search for a way by which your character can set out *seeking* the desired event, person or information. If your character wants something, and works hard to get it, it isn't coincidence anymore.

Having provided your characters with sufficient background and motivation for their actions, and then by making sure coincidence doesn't rule the day, you'll be well along on the way to better story logic. Things will happen for good reason, and your readers will love you for it.

11

Don't Forget Stimulus and Response

STORY LOGIC GOES DEEPER THAN PROVIDING GOOD BACKGROUND MOTIVAtion and avoiding coincidence. Even if you're an ace on these matters, your copy still may be flawed in terms of having things happen for no apparent reason. That's because fiction readers may need more than background and good motive for what their characters do in a story.

Readers will also usually need to see a specific *stimulus* that causes a given *response* right here and now.

The law of stimulus and response dictates that your character must have an immediate, physical cause for what he does. This immediate stimulus cannot be merely a thought inside his head; for readers to believe many transactions, they have to be shown a stimulus to action that is outside of the character—some kind of specific prod that is *onstage right now*.

So for every response you desire in a character, you must provide an immediate stimulus.

Turning this around, it's equally true that if you start by showing a stimulus, then you can't simply ignore it; *you must show a response*.

The law of stimulus and response works at the nitty-gritty level of fiction, line to line, and it also works in melding larger parts of the story. For every cause, an effect. For every effect, a cause. A domino does not fall for no immediate reason; it has to be nudged by the domino next to it.

Let's consider a bit further.

The chapter just before this one looked at character background and plot motivation before mentioning stimulus and response because it's important for you clearly to understand the difference. Background, as we have seen, goes to earlier actions affecting the character's life. Motivation has to do with the character's desires and plans, which grow out of that background, as well as out of what's been going on earlier in the story. Stimulus is much more immediate: it's what happens *right now*, outside the character, to make him do what he's going to do in the next few moments.

For example, if in your story you want your character Martha to walk into the personnel director's office to seek a job, you need some *background* to explain why she needs a job; perhaps she comes from a poor family and has no means of support (long-term background) and maybe she just lost some other job, and so needs a new one right away (short-term background). She has made the decision to apply at this company because she just spent her last few dollars to pay her rent (even shorter-term background, combined with motivation).

Even so, you can't just have Martha sitting there in the office, suddenly get up, and walk into the personnel director's office. In fiction, that won't work; it will seem unreal, incredible. What you have to have is an immediate stimulus to get Martha to get up and walk in *now*.

So you write something like:

> The secretary looked up at Martha and said, "You can go in now." (Stimulus)
>
> Martha got up and walked into the office. (Response)

This is how stimulus-response writing works. It's a bit like a game of baseball. The pitcher throws the ball; the batter swings at the ball. You wouldn't have the pitcher throwing the ball and nobody at the plate swinging at it, would you? And you couldn't have the batter swinging at the ball without a pitcher being out there to throw it, could you?

Strangely enough, novice fiction writers often mess up their copy by doing something almost as obviously wrong as the pitcher-batter mistakes just cited. What happens is that the writer either doesn't know about stimulus-response movement in fiction, or else she forgets it.

The latter error is more common. Almost anyone can see the innate logic of stimulus-response transactions once it is pointed out to them. But in writing, it's amazing how easy it is for some of these same fictioneers to let their imagination get ahead of their logic and see the whole transaction in their mind, *but then forget to provide the reader all the steps*.

My student Wally provided me with a classic example of such forgetfulness once. He wrote:

> Max walked into the room. He ducked just in time.

I looked up from Wally's page and asked, "Why did Max duck? What did he duck? What's going on here?"

Wally scratched his head. "Well, Sally was mad at him. You knew that."

"Wally," I protested, "the fact she was angry is *background*. If I'm to understand why Max ducks, I've got to see an immediate stimulus. Why *did* he duck?"

"She threw a hand mirror at him," Wally said.

"Then you've got to put that in your copy!"

"You mean," Wally said, "I've got to put in *every step*?"

Of course.

Stimulus and response seems so simple, but it's so easy to forget or overlook. I urge you to examine some of your own fiction copy very minutely. Every moment two characters are in interaction, look for the stimulus, then look for the immediate response. Then look for how the other character responds in turn. The stimuli and responses fly back and forth like a Ping-Pong ball, *and no step can be left out.*

And please let me add a few more words to emphasize a point that might otherwise be skimmed over or misunderstood. Stimulus-response transactions—the heart of logic in fiction copy—are *external.* They are played outside the characters, onstage now.

Background is not stimulus.

Motivation is not stimulus.

Character *thought or feeling* is not stimulus.

The stimulus must come from outside, so if put on a stage the audience could see or hear it.

The response that completes the transaction must be outside, too, if the interaction is to continue. Only if the interaction of the characters is to end immediately can the response be wholly internal.

I mention all this because so many of my writing students over the years have tried so hard to evade the precept of stimulus and response. Whenever I explain the procedure in a classroom, it's virtually inevitable that someone will pipe up with, "Can I have the character do something in response to a thought or feeling, without anything happening outside?"

My reply is no, you can't.

Consider: If you start having your character get random thoughts or feelings, and acting on them all the time, the logic of the character and your story will break down. In real life, you might get a random thought for no apparent reason, and as a consequence do or say something. But as we discussed in Chapter Ten, among other places, fiction has to be better than life, clearer and more logical. It is *always* possible to dream up something—some stimulus—that can happen to *cause* the thought or feeling internally, and it is *always* possible to dream up something the responding character can then *do* in the physical sense as the visible, onstage response to the stimulus. Response always follows stimulus onstage now. Response is always caused by a stimulus, onstage now. The fact that there may be some thought or emotional process inside the character between the two events does not mean they both don't always have to be there.

If you find yourself skipping stimuli or responses, or substituting shooting-star internal impulses for stimuli—or failing to show external responses after stimuli—it is certain that your fiction isn't making good sense to the reader. He will complain that, in your stories, things are happening for no reason. And he'll hate your stuff. He may not know why, but he won't believe it.

So, no matter how good you think you are in these logical terms, wouldn't it be a good idea to take just a few minutes someday soon and comb over your copy to make doubly sure?

12

Don't Forget Whose Story It Is

VIEWPOINT.

That's what this section—and the one to follow—are all about.

Viewpoint is perhaps the most-discussed aspect of fiction, yet the one most often screwed up. But perhaps you will never have serious technical problems with the technique of viewpoint again if you will simply follow the advice that heads this page.

Figure out whose story it is.

Get inside that character—and stay there.

That's all there is to it. Except that in its simplicity, viewpoint has many angles to its application.

I'm sure you realize why fiction is told from a viewpoint, a character inside the story. It's because each of us lives our real life from a single viewpoint—our own—and none other, ever. The fiction writer wants her story to be as convincing and lifelike as possible. So she sets things up so that readers will experience the story just like they experience real life: from one viewpoint inside the action.

Each of us is the hero of his own life. The next time you are in a group of people, take a moment to realize how you see everything and everyone around you as interesting—but essentially as role players *in your life*. Then try to observe others around you . . . try to imagine how each of them sees the scene in exactly the same way, from their own unique and centrally important viewpoint.

If fiction is to work, your central character has to experience the story action this way too. How do you as the writer make it happen? Very simply by showing all the action from inside the head and heart—the thought, senses and emotions—of the person you have chosen as the viewpoint character.

It matters not whether you choose to write the story first person: "*Worried, I walked down the lonely street. . . .*" or third person: "*Worried, she walked down the lonely street.*" The device is the same. You let your reader experience everything from inside that viewpoint character.

In short fiction there will usually be a single viewpoint per story.

Changing viewpoint in a short story, where unity of effect is so crucial, usually makes the story seem disjointed. In a novel, there may be several viewpoints, but one must clearly dominate. That's because every story is ultimately one person's story above all others, just as your life story is yours and yours alone. It's a fatal error to let your viewpoint jump around from character to character, with no viewpoint clearly dominating, in terms of how much of the story is experienced from that viewpoint. Life isn't like that. Fiction shouldn't be, either.

To put this in other words: even in a novel of 100,000 words, well over 50 percent—probably closer to 70 percent—should be clearly and rigidly in the viewpoint of the main character. That character's thoughts, feelings, perceptions and intentions should unmistakably dominate the action. When you change viewpoint—if you must—it should be only when the change in viewpoint serves to illuminate for readers the problems of the main viewpoint character.

Where do you put the viewpoint? The easy and obvious answer is that you give the viewpoint to the character who will be in all the right places to experience the crucial stuff in the plot. (It's pretty clear, for example, that if you want to tell the story of a mountain-climbing expedition in Tibet, you can't very well put the viewpoint inside a child who never gets outside of Topeka, Kansas.)

Beyond this point, however, other factors must be considered. Readers like to worry through their stories. They'll worry most about the viewpoint character. And what are readers likely to worry about most? *Whether the character with the most important goal will reach that goal.* Therefore it follows that you should give the viewpoint to the character who has the goal motivation that makes the story go . . . the character who will be in action toward some worthwhile end . . . the story person with the most to win or lose in the story action.

This character—the one threatened at the outset who vows to struggle—will be the character who ultimately is most *moved* by what takes place. That's why some fiction theorists say the viewpoint should be invested in the character who will be most changed by the story action.

It has been pointed out, however, that it's an inevitable result in fiction that the viewpoint character and the moved character will become one and the same. If you don't start out planning your story that way, it will either end up that way—or the story will be a flop. Because the viewpoint character is the focus of all the story's actions and meanings, the viewpoint character *must* become the moved character; it can be no other way.

What does this mean for you as a writer working with viewpoint? For one thing, it means that you simply can't write a story in which the viewpoint is put inside a neutral observer. It won't work. Even in a novel like *The Great Gatsby*, the character Gatsby ultimately is not the most important character. Nick Carraway is the one who is finally moved . . . changed . . . made to see a different vision of the world, and so decides to go back to the Midwest at the end of the story. Nick is the narrator, the viewpoint character, and finally the story is his, and the meaning derived from his sensibilities, whatever the novel may be titled.

To sum up, then, this is what I meant when I say you mustn't forget whose story it is:

- Every story must be told from a viewpoint inside the action.
- Every story must have a clearly dominant viewpoint character.
- The viewpoint character must be the one with the most at stake.
- Every viewpoint character will be actively involved in the plot.

Probably since the dawn of time, beginning writers have wrestled with these principles, hoping to find a way around them. They seem harsh and restrictive. But after you have worked with them a while, you will find them to be very useful in focusing your story. A storyteller has plenty to worry about without wondering whose story it is, or from what vantage point the reader is supposed to experience the story! And, even more to the point from a practical standpoint, you might as well accept viewpoint as a central—perhaps *the* central—device of fiction. You can't escape it. It's simply at the center of how fiction works on readers.

13

Don't Fail to Make the Viewpoint Clear

LET'S SUPPOSE YOU'RE WRITING A STORY ABOUT BOB, AND YOU HAVE DECIDED that he is the viewpoint character. How do you make sure that your handling of his viewpoint is as powerful as it can possibly be?

The first thing you must do is imagine the story as it would seem to Bob, and only to him. Here you really get to exercise your imagination.

As you write the story, you the writer must *become* Bob. You see what he sees, and nothing more. You know what he knows, and nothing more. You hear only what he hears, feel only the emotions he feels, plan only what he can plan, and so on. When you start a scene in which Bob walks into a large room, for example, you *do not* imagine how the room looks from some god-like authorial stance high above the room, or as a television camera might see it; you see it only as Bob sees it, coming in . . . perhaps first being aware only of the light from the far windows glaring in his face, then noticing how warm the air is, then becoming aware of the blurry sea of faces in the audience, then detecting an interior nudge of apprehension, then thinking, "*I'll convince these people that my opinion is right.*"

If you'll stop to ponder it a moment, you'll see that this imaginative linking with your viewpoint character not only makes the story more like real life, but also makes your creative task somewhat easier. You don't have to know what Sally in the back room is seeing or thinking. All that kind of complication is out of Bob's awareness, and therefore out of the story. All you have to do is track along with Bob, and make his experience of the scene as vivid and meaningful as you can.

Having once gotten yourself thoroughly into Bob's viewpoint, however, you need to go a bit further in terms of technique. You need to keep reminding your readers who the viewpoint character is.

To that end, you constantly use grammatical constructions that emphasize Bob's seeing, hearing, thinking, etc.

For example, you would not write something like, "The meeting room for the speech was stuffy." Instead, you would phrase the statement to emphasize that it's Bob's awareness: "Bob felt the stuffy heat of the room close around him and knew he had to make a good speech to hold this audience."

By using clauses like "Bob *felt*" and words like "knew," the writer is showing unequivocally that we are in Bob's viewpoint. Only Bob can know how he feels. Only Bob can know for certain what he is seeing or noticing at that moment. This leads to reader identification with Bob, which is vital if the reader is to have a sense of focus.

Notice, too, that by establishing a relationship between the environment (the hot, crowded room) and the viewpoint (Bob), the professional writer goes on to set up a cause-effect relationship between the outside world from Bob's viewpoint and his interior, feeling-thinking life. Bob goes in, makes some observations, and as a result realizes he has to make the speech of his life. Thus the setting isn't just a static thing being examined for no reason; it has importance; it affects how Bob is feeling; as a result, he is going to *act* somewhat differently.

This movement, from outside the viewpoint character to inside that same character, is at the heart of moment-to-moment motivation in fiction. It is also a very powerful characterization device. You the writer can show the outside world from a viewpoint; then, by relating that outside view to some internal reaction inside your character—which only your character can possibly know—you can share your first little secret with the reader as to what kind of a person this viewpoint character really is.

Does that make sense? Look at it this way: What if Bob's internal response, above, had been to feel amused? Abused? Frightened? Justified? Arrogant? In each case, this single shown response *would change his characterization.*

By picking a viewpoint and emphasizing it constantly, in other words, you do more than usefully limit your authorial problems, and you accomplish more even than making the story lifelike . . . and building sympathy for the viewpoint character. In addition to these benefits, you give yourself another powerful tool for showing your readers who and what your viewpoint character really is . . . in his heart of hearts, in that secret place within himself where there can be no lies or deception.

Of course the converse of what we've just been talking about is also true. You must not only establish and reiterate the viewpoint constantly with the proper kinds of constructions, but you must also make sure that nothing slips into your copy by accident that might lead the reader to assume the viewpoint has moved anywhere else.

If Bob is still your viewpoint character, for example, but you want to show that his boss, Max, is worried about the speech Bob is about to give, you *cannot* throw in a sentence like, "Max was worried about the speech." That construction implies that we are momentarily in Max's viewpoint.

How do we get around the problem? Two possibilities come immediately to mind:

"As he walked to the podium, Bob remembered how worried Max had said he was about the speech."

Or:

"Walking to the podium, Bob glanced at Max and saw the worried frown on his face."

In either case, we've conveyed the information about Max's worry without risk of losing our reader's sense of where the viewpoint is.

You would do well, I think, to test yourself on how you handle viewpoint, since it's such a vital technique in fiction. Here's one way you can do it.

Select a few pages of your own fiction copy. Then go through it with colored pencils and mark it up as follows:

Underline the name of your viewpoint character in red.

Underline in red every statement that clearly defines that character's viewpoint ("He saw," "she heard," "he thought," "she felt," "he intended" and the like).

Look for any intended or accidental statements establishing any other viewpoint. If you find a second viewpoint, underline that character's name in green, and then underline in the same color all the words that establish his viewpoint.

At this point, if you have found more than one viewpoint, *get it out of there*! Rewrite, if necessary, to make it all a single viewpoint.

Learning to handle viewpoint well is a crucial step for any fiction writer. It can be troublesome at first, but later it becomes second nature. That's good, because learning it is a necessity. For without good handling of viewpoint, your readers may forget whose story it is—and you might, too!

14

Don't Lecture Your Reader

THERE YOU ARE, DEEP IN YOUR STORY SOMEWHERE, AND YOU REALIZE THAT there's some vital information that your readers really ought to know. So you write something like:

> Charlie had no way of knowing this, but it is a well-documented fact that Type A personalities suffer a high incidence of heart attacks, and his enemy Sam was definitely a Type A personality. Sam's troubles had begun early in his life, and an examination of his early background provides an interesting example of how compulsive Type A behavior can be destructive. . . .

It's probably pretty obvious to you that this kind of lecture doesn't fit very well into contemporary fiction. There was a time, in the earliest days of the novel, and before the modern short story had begun to assume its present form, when a fiction writer could address "You, dear reader," and speak author-to-reader like a stage lecturer might speak to an audience. But fiction has become much more sophisticated since those long gone days, and readers now won't stand for lectures by the author.

Why? For at least two reasons: First, lectures by the author violate every principle of viewpoint, as just discussed in the two preceding chapters; second, such lectures completely stop the forward movement of the story, and so distract the reader from the plot, where he should be focused.

Another possible reason for avoiding author lectures in your fiction: you may find yourself deviating from the fictioneer's goal—the telling of a story—to that of a pamphleteer, which is trying to sell a belief. Fiction *may* convince readers about some moral, ethical or political issue, but if it does, the convincing is a by-product of the tale-telling. Fiction does not exist primarily to convince anybody of anything; it exists to tell a story, and by so doing to illuminate the human condition.

Let me make a suggestion: if you ever find yourself saying that you are writing a story to "prove" something political or whatever, shelve that story instantly, and don't work on it again until you can write it for its own sake.

Of course writers of fiction care about issues of the day. Often they have very, very strong opinions. But the *published* writers entertain. They don't write to prove anything. If their story happens incidentally to say something thematic, that's grand. Most stories do end up implying some idea or feeling. But the convincing—if any happens—is a by-product of the storytelling process, and cannot be its goal or the story almost certainly will come out like a very bad Sunday sermon rather than as a story.

So perhaps you have been convinced not to try to use fiction as a delivery system for your opinions. A soapbox is better. But what about those inadvertent, well-meaning technical slips that might also read like a lecture in your copy?

These are sometimes harder to catch. As we've mentioned in Chapters Twelve and Thirteen, you'll establish a viewpoint and write in such a way as to remind the reader often where that viewpoint is. It should be relatively easy for you to slip in material that you the author want in the story *as long as the viewpoint character needs to think about it.*

What do I mean here? Simply this: Faced with the need to work some factual material into her story, the good writer does *not* say, "How can I get this into the story?" Instead, she asks herself, "Why does my viewpoint character need to learn (or recall) this information?" Or, "How can I get the viewpoint character to notice what I want noticed here?" Which is quite different from sitting back as the author and shoveling in data.

The more you practice your handling of viewpoint, the easier and more like second nature it will become. The more solidly you're writing in viewpoint, the less likely it is that you'll launch into a distracting lecture by the author.

Look for lectures in your fiction. They tend to be chunks of information that you the writer stuck in there because of what *you* wanted in the story—rather than what the viewpoint character would be thinking or dealing with. If or when you find such obtrusive chunks of author intervention, figure out how to get them in through the viewpoint.

Ask yourself such questions as:

- What can happen in the story to make my viewpoint character remember this?
- What can happen to make my viewpoint character seek out and get this information in the story "now"?
- What other character might come in to tell this information to my viewpoint character—and why?
- What other source can my viewpoint character come upon to bring out this desired information? (A newspaper story, for example, or TV news bulletin.)

There are always ways you can devise to avoid dumping information into the story via the author lecture route. There are always ways . . . and you must always find one of them.

•

15

Don't Let Your Characters Lecture, Either!

AS DISCUSSED IN CHAPTER FOURTEEN, IT ISN'T A GOOD IDEA TO DUMP FACTUAL information into a story via the author-intrusion route. Sometimes writers realize this, but unfortunately decide to use their characters as mouthpieces for the desired data, making the characters lecture at one another in a totally unrealistic way.

Usually dialogue is not a good vehicle for working in research information. Characters tend to make dumb speeches for the author's convenience, rather than talking like real people do. While dialogue does convey useful information in a story—and a lot of it—dialogue's primary function is not to give the author a thinly disguised way of dumping his lecture notes.

Maybe you know the kind of lecture dialogue I mean:

> Charlie walked up and said, "Why, hi there, Molly McBride, who was born in Albany in 1972, of poor but hardworking parents, your father was a store clerk! How nice you look today, wearing that red blouse that goes so nicely with your shoulder-length blond hair! My goodness, as I recall, you must still be married to Brad, the world-champion tennis player, whose last tournament appearance saw him reach the semifinals at Flushing Meadow, where—"

This kind of nonsense is every bit as obtrusive and dumb as the direct author lecture discussed in Chapter Fourteen.

Dialogue emphatically is *not* made up of sequential lectures by various characters intent on telling each other what they already know. Dialogue simply cannot be used as a disguise for author lectures. You the writer must find more clever ways of working your needed information into the story.

Finally, let me make one more impertinent observation about lectures by the fiction author. A large percentage of the information you think must go into your story will find its way into the characters' lives and actions without your much worrying about it *if it is truly relevant.*

On the other hand, you may need to question whether some of the stuff you want in there is really needed. If the characters don't talk about it, remember it, or act upon it in the course of your plot, how can it really be so important? And if it's just your opinion about something, who cares? Certainly not your reader!

Leave the lectures for the classroom or the Moose Lodge. Write fiction!

16

Don't Let Them Be Windbags

IN THE LAST CHAPTER WE WARNED ABOUT LETTING CHARACTERS LECTURE for the sake of piling information into the story. But that's not the only way writers sometimes mess up their dialogue. Sometimes, without realizing it, they let their characters talk on and on, boringly, becoming windbags.

A windbag, in old-fashioned slang, is a person who talks and talks and talks . . . and talks some more . . . and never lets anybody get a word in edgewise.

Windbags in real life are colossal bores.

In fiction they're even worse.

That's important to remember, because so much of modern fiction is composed of dialogue—characters talking. You can't afford to portray windbag characters all the time, because if you do, your characters will be boring, your dialogue will look more like rampant soliloquies than real people talk, and your story will go right down the tubes.

So you have to write modern dialogue. That means that the only time you can let a story character talk like a windbag is when you *intend* to portray him as a windbag. The great majority of your characters have to be more terse and logical than we often are in real life, if the dialogue on the page is to *appear* realistic.

Which is to say: good, *realistic* story dialogue often has little actual resemblance to the way we really talk every day. It just looks that way.

How do you avoid the dread windbag syndrome?

You must *not*:

- Fill pages with endless, rambling talk.
- Try to substitute speeches for dialogue.
- Allow characters to beat every subject to death.
- Let one character totally ignore what the other is saying.
- Fill your story with talk where nobody wants anything.
- Be literary or classic.
- Produce pages of dull, overlong paragraphs of speechifying.

But what, you may ask, can you do to prevent this sort of thing?

In the first place, recognize that a story conversation should almost always follow the rules of stimulus and response as explained in Chapter Eleven.

Second, whenever possible, set up your dialogue scenes so that they play out "one-on-one," getting rid of other characters (who might interrupt and make the conversation more complicated). Setting up one-on-one dialogues makes life simpler all around. If Joe and Bill are to talk in your story, and you also have Sam and Fred standing around, figure a way to have Sam called to the telephone; Fred decides to go to lunch; *now* you have a one on one between Joe and Bill, and it's easier.

Remember, too, that most of the time your dialogue will become sleek, swift and contemporary if you will just provide your viewpoint character with a *conversational goal*. A viewpoint with a goal—information to be sought, or an opinion to be sold—will tend to keep things moving in a straight line even when the other character is being obstreperous. The strongly goal-motivated talker will not allow pages to fill with rambling talk. He will stick to the point, or keep dragging the conversation back to it. And he won't allow long speeches from anybody; he'll keep insisting on a return to the issues at hand.

Having a conversational goal helps you avoid the impulse to drag dialogue cut endlessly, beating the subject to death, too. If the characters stick to the point—and one of them must insist on doing so—then the conversation not only can't wander too far away; it can't extend past the point of decision on the point at issue.

In this regard, it's vital to make sure both characters are listening. If Character A wants to talk about who stole the money, but Character B simply won't pay any attention, and keeps mumbling about his golf score last weekend, all is lost . . . nothing will make sense or progress. You need to make your dialogue participants listen, then respond directly.

If you fill your story with people who don't want anything, of course, all is lost anyway because there can be no focus, and therefore no linear development.

Sometimes, vaguely realizing that their dialogue is failing, novice writers get cute, witty or classic. They have their characters start mouthing trochaic hexameters, or spewing mouthfuls of classical allusions, or talking in formal riddles or paradigms. You have perhaps seen some of this dreadful stuff in an occasional published story or even book. (Every so often a miracle occurs, and such nonsense gets purchased, but not often enough that you can count on it.) *Nobody* talks like these characters. Maybe Tennyson did, but he was surely the last one. Vast, poetic oceans of verbiage surge and roll, their compound-complex breakers crashing over the gerunds and participles littering the story beach. Terrified of short, simple, direct dialogue that somebody will understand and possibly even like, these overambitious fictioneers ruin their story dialogue.

Simplicity . . . directness . . . goal orientation . . . brevity. These are the hallmarks of modern story dialogue. Nothing else will suffice.

Check the dialogue in your own copy. One of the simplest tests may be visual, and can warn of a possible problem. Look at several pages of your story that contain dialogue. Is the right-hand margin grossly irregular, many of the character statements going only halfway across the page, and others filling only perhaps a line and a half? In newspaper terms, do your dialogue pages show a lot of white space?

If they do, good. If they don't, it may mean that your characters are being too long-winded.

Look, too, for clearly stated goals in the dialogue between your characters. If one or both characters have a goal in mind, they won't tend to wander so far from the point . . . and make speeches.

See if you have small mob scenes that you could simplify by setting up one on ones as we just discussed.

Make sure you're following the rules of stimulus and response as outlined in Chapter Eleven.

Now, it may be that you will occasionally allow a character to ramble briefly in order to make the dialogue appear more realistic; you may even let one character briefly lose the thread of the conversation, and need a repeat of something just mentioned. These are fine little tricks. But they are not the norm. Modern dialogue tends to be brief, punchy, single-issue oriented. Impatient readers demand no less.

In writing a draft of a dialogue scene, you may find yourself with ten points in your mind all at once—aspects or questions or comments that you as the writer know must be in the scene somewhere. Sometimes, in your creative anxiety, you may catch yourself letting a character blurt out long diatribes, listing point after point you had in mind. At the stage of first draft, that may be okay; after all, part of what you're doing is just getting the thoughts down so you can start fixing them.

On revision, however, those multipoint speeches will have to be broken down into much smaller components. More exchanges will have to be devised. A page of gray speech in first draft may become five pages of lively dialogue, half of each right-hand page blank, in the revision.

That will be good.

17

Don't Mangle Characters' Speech

THERE WAS A TIME, NOT SO LONG AGO, WHEN FICTION WRITERS STROVE FOR authenticity in some of their stories by attempting to imitate regional and ethnic dialects and pronunciations by purposely misspelling words in their dialogue. Today such practices have fallen into disfavor. For one thing, it takes a very high degree of skill to depart from standard English in dialogue without unnecessarily distracting the reader. For another, styles simply change, and stories using such devices today often seem quaint and old-fashioned. In addition, the sensibilities of minorities are keener today, and they tend to view such mangling of characters' speech as offensive.

For all these reasons, the use of funny spelling or other typographical devices to indicate minority deviations from standard American speech is frowned upon by most cautious editors, and may earn a rejection for your otherwise admirable story.

Some attempts do get by editors and are published. In one recent story, which won't be identified in order to protect the writer, characters in a small town invariably said "shure" for "sure," and "reely" for "really." Try to pronounce these colorful spellings differently than you pronounce the standard spelling, and you begin to see how absurd specialized lingo can become.

All attempts at specialized dialogue or speech devices are not that silly, but all are very difficult to bring off convincingly. Even trying to create "Britishisms" for a Londoner in your story may look awkward to the reader, or even wrong. British argot and slang change as quickly as does American usage; if you get caught using last year's terminology, your informed reader is going to think you're an oaf—and not like your story.

Strange to say, but danger lurks also in much use of mainstream American slang and colloquialism. All such speech fads change fast; what's trendy today may be already dated by the time your magazine story or book see the light of day. It seems only yesterday that kids said things were "super" or "neat." Later the same things were said to be "awesome" or "out of sight." In the academic world, where slang doesn't go, specialized jargon changes just as fast. Where college professors once talked about "paradigms," they began talking about "models," and where they used to say a certain change would "reverberate," they later said it would "impact." Surely you can think of many similar examples.

The moral? Avoid trendy speech. It will certainly date your story next year, or the year after that. Just read Sinclair Lewis today to see this clearly. A novel like *Babbitt* was on the cutting contemporary edge when it came out many years ago. Now the archaic slang makes much of it read like a museum curiosity.

Words misspelled to indicate offbeat pronunciations, dialogue words full of apostrophes to indicate the dropping of letters, excessively fragmented sentences in character talk, and all such devices of realism are often extremely irritating to editors and would-be readers alike. They sometimes obscure meaning, too. And they distract readers from what's going on in the story, and instead focus them on your verbal gymnastics. An occasional elision and use of standard contractions will suffice to make your dialogue readable and realistic. All attempts at more only court disaster.

Finally, while we're looking at ways your lingo can mess up your story dialogue, please consider another error that beginning writers often make in quest for realism. That's the whole question of profanity and obscenity in character speech.

I am now in my third decade of dealing with young writers. Quite a few over the years have been military veterans. Many of these guys wanted to write fiction based on their experiences in the military. Inevitably, they brought me copy studded with oaths, obscenities, curses, filthy puns and all manner of verbal crud like that which is so prevalent in the military (and in a lot of other fields, for that matter). When I protested that a very great many editors are surprisingly bluenosed about excessive use of "dirty words," my young males always protested vehemently that that, after all, "is the way it is."

I have seldom succeeded in convincing them that dirty talk often looks dirtier on the page than it actually is. I have tried to convince them that such strong words, if they are to be used at all, should be saved for those story situations where a really strong word really is needed to convey the emotion. But I haven't convinced many of that viewpoint, either.

So over the years a steady stream of Army/Navy/Air Force/Marine stories and novels filled with dirty words have winged their way out of Norman, Oklahoma, and its environs, headed for the great literary marts of New York. So far, every one of them—*every one of them*—has failed to sell. And I am convinced that the gross language was the only factor that doomed several.

Most of us let slip a cussword once in a while. A few in a novel are certainly not going to shock anybody. But it's a rare, rare bird who has enough talent to sell a story or novel with a high percentage of those words in it. You might be able to mention several examples of books that prove such realism does get published. I can give you the names of dozens of talented people who never got published at all because they couldn't keep the garbage out of their characters' mouths.

You will make your own decisions about character speech. However, I hope you'll think about the points just raised. Oddball spellings, excessive dropped letters to indicate colloquial mispronunciations, attempts at racial or ethnic dialect, and heavy use of realistic dirty talk all risk offending someone; some you might offend will be editors, who have the checkbooks, and others may be members of honorable American minorities who have already been thoughtlessly battered, verbally and otherwise, for a dozen generations or more. Under such circumstances, is it really necessary?

18

Don't Forget Sense Impressions

WALLY, MY PROBLEM STUDENT, BROUGHT ME SOME STORY DIALOGUE THE other day. It read like this:

"Don't make me go any closer!" Annie cried.
"There's nothing to fear," Joe soothed. "See?"
"That's easy for you to say!" quoth Annie.
"Is that better?" asked Joe.
"Oh, yes!" murmured Annie. "Much!"
"Annie, you do love me, after all!"
"Yes!"

I'll spare you the details of the real-life conversation that then ensued between me and Wally. However, the gist of it from my standpoint was that I as a fiction reader didn't have any idea of what was going on in Wally's story in the dialogue just quoted. Wally protested that he had, after all, followed the rules of stimulus and response, and had given me *everything* the characters said; therefore, he couldn't understand what my problem was.

I then tried to explain to Wally that the dialogue left me at a loss. Among other things, I could not:

- *See* anything that was happening during the dialogue;
- *Hear* anything except the dialogue words;
- *Smell* anything that might be pertinent, *Taste* anything, *Feel* any other possible tactile sensations;
- *Know any thoughts* the viewpoint character might be having, so that I might as a reader get a hint as to how I was supposed to be taking this dialogue;
- *Feel any emotions* of the viewpoint character, also as an aid to my reader response to the situation being portrayed;
- *Be aware of the goal* of the viewpoint character, so that I can guess how things are going in the scene.

"Wally," I concluded, "dialogue without any sense impressions, thoughts or feelings of the viewpoint character gets totally abstract; it stops making sense; the reader gets lost. I'm not suggesting great, purple patches of stuff—just enough to keep me oriented."

Wally went off and rewrote. He soon came up with something like the following (his additional material is italicized):

> *The chill wind tugged at Joe's coat as he pulled Annie closer to the edge of the cliff. Behind them, gusts swayed the ponderosa pines. A few feet from where he now led the quaking girl, the granite escarpment simply stopped. Beyond the brink was the windy vastness of a sheer, thousand-foot drop, straight down.*
>
> *Annie's shaking became more violent, and her eyes glistened with sudden, frightened tears.* "Don't make me go any closer!"
>
> *Joe stepped back a step, leaving her alone on the brink. He had to make her confront this terror or she could never forget what had happened here last summer.* "There's nothing to fear," Joe soothed. "See?"
>
> *Annie's wide eyes took in the space between them—how much farther back from the edge he had moved, leaving her alone.* "That's easy for you to say!" she said bitterly.
>
> *Suddenly Joe couldn't be cruel to her any longer. He stepped forward and wrapped his arms around her, intent only on protecting her, always, if she would just let him.* "Is that better?" he asked.
>
> "Oh, yes!" Annie murmured *gratefully, snuggling against him.* "Much!" *Still crying, she raised her face to his and gently kissed him. Her perfume, mountain flowers, surrounded them. Joe could scarcely believe the glad certainty that swept through him. She clung more fiercely.*
>
> *Her response told Joe everything he needed to know. Her fear was gone in this instant, and so was his worry that she had never really cared for him.* "Annie," *he said, touching her face with his fingertips,* "you do love me, after all!"
>
> *Annie sobbed and buried her face against his chest.* "Yes!"
>
> *Her fear was gone. But Joe knew he had won far more than the battle against her past. Still holding her close, he led her back off the cold, windy cliff and into the sea-green shade of the woods. . . .*

I thought then—and still think—that my student Wally might have overdone it a bit with his revision. But he put in some sense impressions and thoughts, as well as intentions and an indication of emotions. As a result, I the reader now saw where we were, could somewhat sense the physical impressions of the place, knew what viewpoint Joe wanted, and why he was acting as he was, understood a little of Annie's plight and emotions—and in general *could get involved.*

Sure, student Wally might need to tone it down a bit on final rewrite. But he was now on track, writing dialogue the reader could follow.

If this episode with Wally rings any kind of bell with you, I urge you to examine your own dialogue in a story. You must not make your readers deaf or blind. You must provide them with sense impressions from the viewpoint character. And you must tell them some of what the viewpoint character wants, thinks and feels emotionally, too. Otherwise the dialogue will get as meaningless—and float in as abstract a space—as Wally's did in first draft.

Of course there will be times when the dialogue transaction, or other story action, is very simple and straightforward, and the challenge to you the writer will be easy because you won't have to put down very much to keep the reader oriented. But there will be other situations where the movement of the characters, the complexity of the setting, or the depth of the viewpoint character's thoughts, feelings and changing motives may require considerably more author interpretation than Wally's did. In other words, how much you put in, in addition to the dialogue, may depend on how complicated the transaction becomes.

In any case, however, you can't ask your reader to play blind man's bluff. Just because you see and hear details in your imagination as you write the scene does *not* mean that the reader will by some magic guess the same details. You have to give her enough hints to go on.

Perhaps you will want to check some of your own recent fiction copy at this point to see if you have provided enough sense-emotion-thought detail to keep readers oriented during the flow of the dialogue.

19

Don't Be Afraid to Say "Said"

THERE WAS ANOTHER POINT TO BE MADE ABOUT STUDENT WALLY'S DIALOGUE as shown in the preceding chapter. It's such a basic point—but one so often misunderstood—that it deserves a chapter of its own.

"How do I say somebody in my story said something?" students ask again and again.

"Use the word 'said,' " I usually tell them, "and for heaven's sake put the noun or pronoun first."

In the example in Chapter Eighteen, Wally violated both rules. He used every word *but* "said" as an attribution verb, and for some unknown reason he turned his syntax around so he was writing things like "quoth Annie"—the verb first.

Reverse order attribution is not a biggie; some fine authors do it a lot. I have known editors, however, who got very irritated with "said he" and "replied she" rather than the more straightforward way of ordering the words; they say the reverse order sounds old-fashioned to them, and is distracting.

Sometimes, of course, reverse order is almost mandatory, as when you have to get a long title or description in with the name. You may find yourself confronted with something like:

> "I'm tired of arguing," Joe Smith, aging family patriarch and president of the First Mercantile Bank of Lake City, Colorado, said.

In such a case, to get away from that "said" yipping along a block behind the quote, you'll probably use reverse order, and rightfully so, getting the "said" in right behind the quoted words and in front of everything else. But most transactions are simpler, and standard order seems to be the norm.

As to the other matter—use of synonyms for the simple attribution word "said"—I really believe things are more serious. "Said" is a transparent word—a pointer to a who who said something. Any other attribution word will stick out and perhaps distract the reader without need, unless the situation really does demand a "scream" or a "sigh" or a "shout." You should use the invisible word "said" about 90 percent of the time. Of course you will use other words like "asked," "replied," "told," etc.—when the context makes such a word obviously appropriate. But you should use even these only when it really does seem natural in context.

If you've been guilty of using every synonym in the thesaurus, using the simple "said" will worry you to death for a while. It's one of those "author worries" that readers just don't think about. Believe me: If you use stage action and thoughts, and the simple verb "said," readers will be totally happy. Why distract them and wear out your thesaurus when it's not required or even smart?

Take some time to think about this one. Examine your copy critically. Are you *sure* the reader is going to be oriented in the ways we've discussed here? And have you fine-checked your dialogue to make sure it doesn't sound old-fashioned or eccentric? From such distinctions good writers are made; care for the reader, along with standard usages, free you to concentrate on characters and plots—the really good stuff of fiction.

20

Don't Assume You Know; Look It Up

ALL OF US GO THROUGH LIFE ASSUMING WE UNDERSTAND SOME THINGS THAT we really don't. You may *think* you know how to change a tire, but until you've had to do it on the side of a narrow road in a driving rainstorm, you can't be sure. Similarly, you may *think* you know all about some factual material that you're putting in your story, but—again—maybe you really don't.

"Gee, but I want to write fiction so I don't have to mess with facts!" you may say.

Nope. Wrong motivation. If you get a fact wrong in your story, somebody is going to notice it. Maybe the editor considering your story—maybe a thousand readers who notice it and complain to your editor after the yarn is published.

In either case, the end result will be similar to what can happen when you don't know how to change a tire beside the road: you might end up feeling like you've been run over by a truck.

Take it from one who learned the hard way. Once, long ago, in the earliest days of my writing career, I was writing a western novel. I gave my cowboy a Colt single-action revolver, a "Peacemaker" model, which he referred to as a thumb-buster.

The novel was set in 1868.

The Colt single-action model I described was not patented until 1872.

My editor missed it. You should have seen some of the irate letters I got from western history buffs—some of whom probably never bought another novel written by me.

An error of fact can not only make you look foolish. It can destroy your readership and your relationship with an editor. You simply cannot guess or assume you know. Even when you are 99 percent sure, *look it up*!

In one of my writing classes, I hand out a sheet with actions listed, and ask the students to tell me what would happen immediately following each action I've listed, stimulus-response fashion. One of the actions reads as follows:

He shoved the throttle of the plane to the fire wall.

Now, I ask them, what happens next?

Some blithely assume that a throttle on an airplane works like a throttle control on a tractor, or as it did on old automobiles, i.e., that pushing the throttle in will cut the engine to idle. (They may not know what the fire wall is, either, but they usually guess correctly that that's an airplane term for the instrument panel.) Anyway, not asking me for factual input, they guess—and write something like:

The plane's engine slowed.

Which would make the plane slow down if on the roll, or its nose dip sharply if it was in the air.

Unfortunately, that's 100 percent wrong. When you shove the throttle forward on a plane, you speed the engine. What would happen (assuming the engine was running and it didn't backfire or something awful):

The engine roared to full power.

Which would make the plane start rolling or speed up if already rolling on the ground, or its nose rise and/or speed increase if in the air.

So guessing in this case—trusting to analogous experience—often leads careless student-takers of this exercise to put down absolutely the opposite of what is accurate. And if you put something dumb like this in your story, you can be sure a lot of people will notice the error, think it's dumb, and *assume everything else in the story might be wrong, too*. And there goes your readership, and maybe your future as a writer.

Even if factual errors weren't this dangerous, you ought to have more professional pride than to guess. Few people live out of range of a public library. Most librarians will bend over backwards to help you research a point; the harder the search, the more they're likely to get challenged and work with you. Don't be afraid to ask for help.

Research can be fun. It's necessary. And—although until you experience this you may find it hard to believe—it can help you come up with lots of great new plot and character ideas.

Here's an example. Once, while writing a novel called *The Winemakers*, I made several trips to California for firsthand interviews and on-site research in the Napa Valley. During my writing of the third draft of the book, I went back once more to interview a particularly colorful vintner I had missed on earlier visits. At the same time, in the back of my mind was the fact that I wasn't satisfied with the opening of my novel; it lacked tension.

Touring the winemaker's facility, I walked with him behind some large stainless steel tanks where white wine was being fermented at a cool temperature. There were electrical cables on the floor, and the owner cautioned me to step over them carefully. "Those go to a computer that baby-sits the wine and controls the cooling," he told me. "If those get pulled out, we could be in real trouble."

Bingo! Instantly—because I was there researching something else entirely—I had the opening of the novel as it was later published: a scene where a winemaker enters the winery early one morning, and finds that a saboteur has pulled out the wires.

As you continue your writing career, you may find that there are books or maps or whatever that you go back to again and again. You may decide to begin building a modest research library. Mine includes a huge book of maps of countries around the world; many Michelin and Fodor's travel guides; gun catalogues and blueprints; everything I've ever seen on the KGB, CIA, FBI and similar organizations; two encyclopedias of world history; a guide to popular songs, plays, movies and books on a year-by-year basis since early in the century, and many others. Your needs may be radically different. Whatever they may be, and whether you build your own little library or not, never guess. Take the time to look it up!

21

Don't Ever Stop Observing and Making Notes

YOU MUST NEVER STOP WORKING ON YOUR KEENNESS OF OBSERVATION. HONing your ability to observe accurately—and to write down what you've noticed—must be part of your lifelong commitment to fiction.

If you've been writing any time at all, of course, I'm sure you feel that you are an accurate observer, and a skillful writer of whatever you observe. Most of us, however, need to stand back from ourselves occasionally to make sure we haven't become lazy or passive in how we relate to the real world which is our story material.

Let me suggest a couple of simple exercises you should do carefully from time to time—not only to check up on yourself for continuing keenness of observation, but to keep your skills polished.

Look at that tree in your backyard, or in the nearby park. *Really* look at it. What color is it? Green? What *shade* of green? How is its color different from the elm nearby, or that blue spruce across the way? What shape is it? Round? Tall and graceful in the breeze, like a young ballerina, or bent with age and disease, like an old crone broken by life in the streets? How does it stand out in its surroundings? Is it tall and stark black against the eye-hurting brilliance of a summer sun? Gently fuzzy and soft in the evening twilight? Dark and frightening, casting black shadows of fear from the corner street lamp? How would *you* describe it in a few words, to make a picture of it leap to life in your reader's mind?

Or suppose you meet a new person today, or happen to pass a stranger on the street. Instantly you form some impression of that person. Immediately you begin to draw conclusions about what kind of person he or she is. In real life, casually, you make perhaps dozens of observations in an instant; then you draw conclusions from them. For a nonwriter, such a process is automatic and unexamined. But for you the fiction writer the process must be made conscious, then examined and related to your work.

Look at that new person. Force yourself to note details actively and consciously, rather than passively and unconsciously. What details are you looking at first? Second? Only later? What details are you using as a basis for assumptions about what kind of person this is? Note body conformation, height, weight, clothing, hair, facial expression, stance, skin coloration, movement of eyes, gestures, speed of movement, age, tone of voice, loudness of voice, accent if any, intonation, speed of speaking, vocabulary. When the person begins speaking, note too what his topic may be; his characteristic attitude—whether happy, sad, angry, frightened, bitter, cynical, hopeful, trusting, whatever; note his speaking cadence, pitch and rhythms.

As soon as you can, make notes of everything you have observed. Do you note some "hole" in your observations, some detail you didn't pick up that you now wish you had? Do you find yourself wishing you could go back and look again? Do you find that your notes might describe some other tree or some other vague and ordinary person? If you experience any of these reactions, you probably need to observe more consciously. Just knowing that you need to do this—and remembering not to fall back into routine, passive experiencing—will make you more alert and better as an observer.

Having made your observations and notes, however, you as a writer of fiction must always take another step, that of relating your observations to the writing process.

Here is what I mean. Suppose you just met a new person, and found her interesting, striking or unusual in some way. (If you observed keenly enough, you *always* will find a new acquaintance to be one of the above.) Now ask yourself: "How can I write down my description in such a way that it becomes even more vivid and striking than what I just observed?"

Then write it!

As discussed in Chapter Seven, you won't ever take a real person literally from life and put her in your fiction; real people, no matter how well portrayed, just aren't big and unusual enough for good fiction. But your work in observing and writing real people or places as vividly as possible will make you a far better writer, and even more interesting when you fictionalize your observations.

One additional point: it will be instructive for you to write down everything you notice, in as much detail as possible, in your note-taking phase. "Looking for more words" (as one of my students once put it) prods you to look broader and deeper sometimes. When you practice your final writing of this information, however, you should ask yourself what few details might stand out for the whole—how briefly you can write your description or data, and still provide the reader with a vivid picture.

In this process of *distilling* the impressions into final written form, you should watch out for adjectives and adverbs. Some will be necessary, but if you find yourself stringing them together like sausages, you must realize that you are no longer writing vivid copy. Good writing of this kind is lean and terse. It thrives on brevity, directness, simplicity, concreteness, contrast—precise, specific nouns and strong verbs. If you string out adjectives in an attempt to get the job done, your reader will go to sleep. Adjectives, like adverbs, are lazy words, slowpokes, tranquilizers. Watch out for them!

The more you force yourself consciously to observe and note details you can use—and the more you practice actually writing descriptions and factual passages so that they are as striking and evocative as possible—the keener you will become in picking up data, and the better you will become in learning to use it to improve your writing.

It's a multi-step process, you see:

- *First*, you stop being passive and actively examine your environment.
- *Second*, you seek out what makes this tree . . . this person . . . unique.
- *Third*, you go through the formal process of recording your observations so you won't lose them.
- *Fourth*, you practice translating your observations into deft, brief, evocative writing.

This whole process is a great deal of fun. Writers who practice it—and that includes all professionals—find that it makes them feel more alive, more in touch with everything and everyone, more excited about living. The job of recording observations, then writing them as brilliantly as possible, keeps them constantly alert and challenged—stimulated by new ideas and associations—and improving in the clarity and impact of their style.

Many fiction writers put much of this kind of work in their journals. A journal can include many kinds of writing and information. But often this sort of thing dominates such a volume.

Try working on your own skills in this way. Make it a lifetime habit. You will never be bored, you will always be challenged, and you are sure to grow.

22

Don't Ignore Scene Structure

THE TENSE, CONFLICTFUL SECTIONS OF YOUR STORY ARE THE PARTS THAT most excite and intrigue your readers. For that reason, you should play out those parts of your story for all they're worth.

How do you do that? You put it onstage in the story *now*, and you develop the action between the characters moment by moment, with nothing left out; you follow the rules of cause and effect, stimulus and response. To put this another way: you make sure that you never summarize during a high point of conflict in your story.

The result of moment-by-moment handling is a segment of your story which is just like life; there's no summary there, obviously.

Most professionals call such a part of their story *a scene*. However they may differ in defining how a scene works, they tend to agree on the major point just emphasized: you must never summarize while writing a scene. Not only does moment-by-moment development make the scene seem most lifelike; it should also be noted that it's in a scene where your reader gets most of his excitement. If you summarize, your reader will feel cheated—shortchanged of what he reads for—without quite knowing why.

Let's look at the structure of a scene just a bit more to make sure you understand how it works and why summary is lethal to its effectiveness.

To have conflict, you have to have two people with opposing goals. They have to want the same thing, or Character A must want to thwart Character B's immediate goal-motivated quest. Therefore, to start a scene, the first thing you have to do is have one of your characters (usually the viewpoint character) clearly state or show what it is he wants. Once that goal has been demonstrated ot stated *with complete clarity* so the reader can have no doubt about what's at issue, then the other character to be in the scene must say, in effect, "Oh, no you won't"—and start the fight.

The fight, the conflict, makes up the bulk of the scene. If it's over a simple issue, the scene may take only a couple of pages to play for all it's worth, although most scenes tend to run a little longer than that. In this portion, the characters try different tacks, varying arguments; they struggle for the upper hand. They *do not* just stand there, in effect yelling at each other "Yes, I can!" and "No, you can't!" Every step of their maneuvering is covered in detail.

In a dialogue scene (the most common kind), the maneuvers are verbal. In an action scene, the maneuvers might involve a destroyer crisscrossing over a submarine, trying to hit it with depth charges. In any case, one goal-motivated entity tries something; the other parries and tries something else; the first entity responds with still another stab. And so on, back and forth, no summary, following the rules of stimulus and response.

While this struggle takes place, the readers are bound to worry. While they might worry about a lot of things, the main thing they'll worry about is the *scene question*.

What's the scene question? It's the inversion of the stated scene goal.

Here's what I mean. If you start a scene by having the destroyer commander say, "We have to sink that sub!" Readers will turn the goal statement into a scene question: "*Will they sink the sub?*"—and worry about it. If you start your scene with the young woman saying, "Mr. Jones, I have come to ask you for a job," your readers will turn that stated goal into a question, and worry whether the heroine will get the job she wants. Readers are willing to worry about virtually any scene goal, as long as you make clear to them that the goal is vital to the character's story quest.

To put this another way: If the stated scene goal is clearly relevant to the character's *story goal*, it will be vital to that character's happiness and the outcome of the story. If the scene goal is relevant in this way, readers will see how important the outcome of the scene is going to be and will worry about it.

The conflict portion of the scene draws readers out through a moment-by-moment drama, extending the scene suspense with pleasurable agony.

At some point, of course—after two or six or a dozen pages—the scene must come to an end. If your readers are to feel satisfied, the scene has to end in some dramatic way. Therefore, it can't just stop; it has to provide some new twist or movement for the story.

In addition, the ending of every scene has to be logical; it can't cheat the readers. They have eagerly read the scene, worrying about a question. So to play fair with them, the conclusion of your scene *has to answer the question posed by the goal in the first place*.

So if the question was whether the destroyer would sink the sub, the end of the scene has to answer that question. If the question was whether the woman would get the job, the end of the scene has to tell whether she did or didn't get the job.

To maintain reader tension, however—which you always want to do—you should seldom provide a happy answer to the scene question. Ideally, to keep readers involved and worried, the scene should answer the question with a bad development.

We call this kind of scene ending a *disaster*.

How do you create disaster? Whatever your viewpoint character wants, he must not get it at the end of the scene. For if he does, he has suddenly become happy . . . story tension relaxes . . . the reader goes to sleep . . . and your story has failed.

So, again turning to the example about the destroyer, the captain must not clearly see that he has without doubt sunk the submarine. To the question, "Will the destroyer sink the sub?" the answer must not be a simple and unqualified *yes*. The submarine must escape, or shoot a torpedo through the destroyer before itself sinking, or manage to radio for help. Or possibly the submarine can be sunk, but debris proves *it was a friendly sub*.

Such dynamic bad news keeps the story rolling forward.

Any time you start to write a scene, you should go through the following process:

1. Decide specifically what main character's immediate goal is.
2. Get this written down clearly in the copy.
3. On a separate note somewhere, write down for yourself, clearly and briefly, what the scene question is. Word this question so it can be answered "yes" or "no."
4. In your story, after the goal has been shown, bring in another character who now states, just as clearly, his opposition.
5. Plan all the maneuvers and steps in the conflict between the two characters you have set up.
6. Write the scene moment-by-moment; no summary.
7. Devise a disastrous ending of the scene—a turning of the tables or surprise that *answers the scene question badly*.

After you have practiced this procedure for a short while, I think you'll begin to see that it has within it the essential dynamic of fiction, the way fiction "works." A character wants and strives and is battered back; tension increases, and so does reader sympathy; then the character strives again.

This structure of scene . . . one scene inevitably leading to another scene . . . gives your fiction straight-line development. In addition, the structure powerfully implies something wonderful about life and the human condition. In using scene structure, you show people who struggle and try to take charge of their lives; indirectly, you are saying that people in real life can do that, too. In addition, you imply that life is not merely blind fate . . . that anyone can struggle and try to take their own life by the scruff of the neck, and improve it. Finally, by showing a character meeting serious disaster after such a struggle, then getting up to struggle again, you say something positive about human strength and courage.

Please note, however, that none of this can happen—nothing can work—if the scene does not grab your readers and intensely involve them. To accomplish that, the scene must be lifelike. And the greatest danger to this verisimilitude is summary. Check out the scenes in your story. If you find inadvertent summary, by all means fix it by playing out that part of the scene in detail. Nothing less will do.

23

Don't Drop Alligators Through the Transom

DISASTERS—THOSE BAD TWISTS THAT END SCENES WITH AN UNHAPPY ANSWER to the scene question—often are very bad indeed. But sometimes the use of the word "disaster" confuses a new writer, and she thinks *any* kind of really bad thing will work at the end of a scene.

It is said that somebody once provided a "disaster" at the end of a detective-client scene by literally dropping an alligator through the transom.

In the fabled detective yarn, there sat our Sam Spade clone, interviewing his beautiful client in his grubby office. His goal, clearly stated, was to learn the name of the man who had threatened her life. Thus the scene question clearly was: Would he discover the identity of the man?

At the end of the scene, according to legend, the writer realized she needed a disaster. So *kerplop*! over the transom of the detective's office door came a live alligator, wetly hitting the floor beside the desk and opening wide in a decidedly nasty mood.

The development was pretty stupid in that story. Why? Because it didn't answer the scene question.

The question, remember, was, "Will Sam learn the identity of the man threatening his client?" The alligator had nothing to do with that question.

If so, the disaster had to answer that question. The answer could *not* be, in effect, "Gosh, I don't know about that, but an alligator just fell through the office door transom."

That's the worst kind of cheating, the sorriest kind of writing.

Don't do it. You'll give all of us fiction writers a bad name.

Figure out what the scene question is. Then devise a setback, negative answer for the end of the scene, one that is bad news, logical but unanticipated, *but which answers the question asked.*

In the case of the mythical scene and question just presented, it's hard to imagine how an alligator could provide an honest disaster. But it's easy to think of some disasters that would have worked.

The answer simply could have been: "No, Sam never got an answer."

Better yet, the answer could have been: "Yes, Sam finally got the answer, but when the client identified her threatener, it turned out to be Sam's dearest friend."

Or it might even have been: "No, Sam never got his answer, but his persistence so angered his client that she fired him on the spot, storming out of his office and leaving him *never* to know—or have the income he needed from her fee."

It isn't always easy to figure out the logical but unanticipated disaster. You can do it, though. You must, if you're going to play fair with your readers and keep your story moving forward with tension and suspense.

24

Don't Forget to Let Your Characters Think

IN YOUR ANXIETY TO BUILD YOUR STORY IN A STRAIGHT LINE, WITH TIGHT scene plotting, you may run the risk of plotting action so tightly that your characters never have time to catch a breath.

Are your stories like that? Did anyone ever frown and admit that your story confused them . . . just a little? If so, the chances are good that your story problem lies in your failure to provide time and structure for your characters to breathe . . . and think.

Most writers build components into their yarns to provide this kind of pacing time. Sometimes they may call such a part of their story a "valley." But ultimately this name for breathing time in a story is not very helpful to the writer. Long ago, I heard literature professors talk about high points in fiction as "peaks," and the quieter points as "valleys." And the terminology confused me for years until I finally figured out what they were trying to say.

When they spoke of "peaks," they were talking about *scenes*. For scenes, as discussed in Chapter Twenty-two, represent the high points of excitement, conflict and reader involvement.

When they spoke of "valleys," they were talking about quieter times in the story when conflict was not onstage in the story now—when the character had time to feel emotion, reflect on recent developments, and plan ahead.

We call the "valley" parts of your story the *sequels*.

Sequels, however, are more than just the quiet times in your story . . . more than little spots that provide breathing time for the character and the reader. They are those parts of your tale in which you show your character's reaction to the disaster that just took place . . . then planning what he is going to do next to try to get his quest back on track.

You must not forget to provide such sequels.

Think for a moment about times in your own life when something really bad—some disaster—befell you. What was the pattern of your response?

If it really was a disaster, the first thing you felt, perhaps only for an instant, perhaps for months, was *emotion*.

At some point, however, you stopped feeling blind emotion, and began the process of *thought*.

And at some point you told yourself, in effect, "I've got to get going again . . . I've got to make some *decision*.

This pattern, emotion-thought-decision, is the kernel of the structure of the sequel.

In planning your story's next development after a scene-ending disaster, you must put yourself in the mind and heart of your viewpoint character: imagine her feelings, in all their shadings and ramifications; then go through with her the painful transition into thought, the wondering "What shall I do next?"; finally, imagine with and for her what that new, *goal-motivated decision* ought to be.

Having done this, you will have planned her sequel.

Now, having planned—imagined—her sequel, you ordinarily will write it. How much emotion will you portray? How many pages will you devote to her feelings, before she progresses to thinking? That will depend on the nature of the disaster that just befell her, what kind of character she is, what kind of story you are writing. In a romance, your written delineation of her emotional response may take many pages; in an action story, you may have such plot pressure on her that she must respond in some new action almost at once, without the luxury of taking time for much feeling; with a sensitive heroine you may have to devote pages to her feelings, while with a gruff woman of the world, it may be more realistic if she shrugs off the hurt almost at once, and gets on with business.

The same is true in terms of how much page space you will give to the thinking portion of the sequel. A college professor may take many pages to think logically about what to do or where to go next; another kind of character may make an impetuous decision almost at once.

As you take your character through these parts of her sequel, you may often be inside her head, with no one else around. Or she may talk to a friend or confidante, and "talk out" most of her sequel. In either case, since this is the feeling-thinking part of the story, and not so exciting as the scenes, *you are allowed to summarize*. Thus your character may look back on earlier parts of the story, or of her life. You may have a sentence such as, "She worried about it for four days, and then on Thursday . . ." As you work through your character's reactions and planning almost anything goes in terms of timing.

At some point, however—perhaps sooner, perhaps later—your character must make some new decision in order to get the plot moving forward again. So you move your character to her next decision, her next goal.

And what is that new goal? It's the goal she carries into her next scene!

Scenes end in disasters, which require sequels. Sequels lead inevitably to new decisions based on new experience, and these new decisions involve a new goal. The moment the character acts on this new goal—and encounters new conflict—you are into the resulting next scene.

Thus the major structural components of fiction—scene and sequel—link like the strongest chain. In the scene you provide excitement and conflict, ending in disaster; in the sequel you provide feeling and logic, and the character's decision, which leads directly into the next scene.

In imagining your story, you probably ought to plan every sequel. In writing the final draft of the story, it may be that you will sometimes leave out a sequel in order to speed from one scene directly into the next. Such decisions are based on story type and tactics, and your "fingertip feeling" for how fast or slow the story should be at any given point. The key here is to remember that scenes move swiftly and read fast; sequels tend to move slowly, and read like story "valleys." It follows, then, that if your story feels slow to you, you may need to expand your scenes and cut, or even eliminate, some of your sequels. While if your story seems to be going at an insane pace, with no characterization or logic, you may need to trim some of your scenes a bit, or expand your sequels to provide more breathing room.

If the idea of sequel is new to you, it may help you to study some stories by other writers. Work to pick out the sequels. Notice how the author is often inside the head of a character alone, feeling and thinking about the plot action or other story people. How is the emotion shown? How are the thoughts presented? How does a writer get from random feelings to increasingly linear thought to some firm—if desperate—final decision that will lead to new action?

Try to make every such analysis a learning experience. If it helps, make some notes in your journal, or elsewhere, about how sequels are handled. The analysis will help you enrich your own skills in handling these vital components of story.

25

Don't Wander Around in a Fog

"WAIT A MINUTE; I DON'T KNOW WHAT'S GOING ON HERE."

Did you ever read a short story or novel that gave you this feeling partway through? Worse, did you ever *write* a story where you suddenly started feeling that way?

It's a pretty bad feeling when it comes during a story you're reading. But it's far worse when it happens during your writing of a story. In that case, it probably signals potential disaster.

Of course all of us experience times during first draft when things do not seem to be going well—when all our careful planning seems to have failed us, and the plot no longer seems to work. Sometimes we can muddle through and fix things later. But even if we make a good fix and later sell the story or book, it's not fun to go through.

It just doesn't pay to wander around in a fog when you're supposed to be putting down a story that makes sense. At best it wastes time. At worst, it wrecks your project. Fortunately, there are some things you can do to minimize such times of confusion.

First, you should always begin with a brief statement, as precise as possible, about what your planned story is essentially about.

Second, you should remember always to follow the story, which is to say, the line of conflict growing out of the lead character's goal.

Third, you should beware of late-blooming ideas that seem to come from nowhere during your writing of the project.

Some writers would protest the first advice, saying they "write by inspiration," or "do the story to see how it's going to come out." I hope you're not one of those. The more planning you do before starting to write, the better. Some writers do a detailed outline or proposal; others make elaborate notes on the characters; some make do with a scribbled page or two out of a legal tablet, sketching in a synopsis of the plot. Whatever the individual procedure may be, however, there is a central idea in such planning: *Be sure you know what your story is about before you start.*

This is easy to say and hard to do. One of the reasons it's hard is that all of us tend to imagine a lot more story than we can ever put down in the finished product, the limits of space and time being what they are. Another reason such summary is hard is that the creative imagination likes to freewheel, and detests being forced to boil its ideas down to the ultimate direct simplicity. "If I write down the idea as succinctly as possible," some will cry, "then I won't need to write the story!"

Pardon me while I disagree. As a teacher over the years I've seen far too many stories—shorts and novels alike—founder in midstream because the author simply lost her way—forgot what the original wonderful idea was, in its essence. Writing a novel, for example, is a long and arduous task, and during the composition no writer can keep all the project's aspects in mind all the time. We forget a subplot for a while, or we get overly fascinated with a minor character, or we simply get tired and lose creative focus.

In all such cases, the existence of a brief statement of the story, written when the original vision is clear, can be a lifesaver. I urge you to avoid the fog by producing a story statement.

How long should it be? Absolutely no more than 150 words, and preferably shorter. What should it have in it? The following:

1. The basic plot situation in which the story is to play.
2. The name and identity of the main viewpoint character.
3. This character's story goal.
4. The name of the primary opposition character.
5. What this "villain" wants, and how he opposes the main character.

Dwight V. Swain, noted author and teacher of writing, has written that a sample story summary containing these elements would read something like my following example:

> Hungry and needing money (situation), out-of-work Joe Smith (name and identity) must get a job at Acme Tool Co. (viewpoint character's main goal). But can he get the job when old enemy Sam Jones (primary opposition) tries to waylay him at the plant gate to prevent the job interview? (villain desire and plan).

In this example, of course, we have an idea for a short story of perhaps only one or two scenes. Writing the kernel of a complex novel is much harder. It can be done, however! And boiling off all the secondary aspects of a novel to reveal its skeleton may provide just the tiny reminder you'll need in the throes of a several-hundred-page project.

Before I wrote the first novel in my Brad Smith espionage series I summarized it like this:

> Called back to duty by his former CIA masters, aging tennis star Brad Smith goes to Budapest to try to help a young woman tennis player escape that country. But can he get her out when the CIA plot is foiled, he is alone, and the UDBA is onto his mission?

Now, of course the plot of this 75,000-word novel contained many more questions than this. But precisely because subplotting in this project was so complicated—and there were so many characters ultimately involved—having this "kernel statement" helped me remember what the central thrust of the novel was supposed to be.

Let me urge you to take this sort of step yourself, always.

Having done this, you will be more ready to take the second step that will keep you out of the fog, and that is of *following the story.*

It sounds absurd, doesn't it, to say a writer should follow the story? But stories are often screwed up because the writer forgot . . . or lost . . . this principle. The story is where the conflict is. The conflict grows out of the central viewpoint character's quest after a central goal. If you remember this, you won't get as confused about where your story should go next. You as the author will continually ask yourself: *What is the goal? Where is the conflict?* And write those segments.

Sometimes the temptation is to follow some minor character "because she's interesting." Watch out for such feelings on your part; more often than not, they signal that you've lost the thread of conflict . . . allowed your primary character or characters to get passive. You fix this by giving the main character some new thrust—a plot stimulus—to rekindle the flame of conflict and plunge him into the struggle anew.

Examine your own thinking as you plot and write a story. Are you following the line of conflict? Keeping the main viewpoint character stimulated, involved, moving ahead in his quest? I hope so! If not, look back at your basic statement of what the story was to be about. It contains the basic goal, and the basic conflict, which together define the story question. Get your story moving again, and on the right track, by following that line of struggle.

At some point, of course, you will have done most of the above work as well as you could during one or two drafts. At that time, you will try to lean back from the project a bit and consider ways you might improve it.

This is a necessary and vital part of revising any story of any length. Sometimes flaws are seen and corrected. More often, new angles are detected and worked into the story with a resulting enrichment. For all of that, you should always remember to be a bit leery of any major, far-out plot or character "inspirations" that seem to come out of nowhere at this late stage of the creative process.

That's because your imagination tends to be a fairly short-term tool, and it gets bored easily. Also, it's a lazy facility, and would rather work on some new "game" rather than concentrate long hours or months on the same matter. So what often happens is, the imagination sends up for you some new grand idea that sounds like great fun because it's fresh, *but really has nothing whatsoever to do with the present project.*

So in thinking about revision of your story set in Chicago, you get this brilliant idea for an episode set in Afghanistan; or it suddenly occurs to you in the dead of night that, wouldn't it be neat if your twenty-six-year-old protagonist were changed into a seventy-seven-year-old crone?

Such blinding flashes of "inspiration" may sometimes work. But ninety-nine times out of a hundred, they represent a rebellion by a rambunctious imagination, a *bad* impulse to be avoided like the plague. If you have planned your story and written through it, following the conflict, major deviations from your plan at the late stage of revision will at best represent enormous and dangerous rewrite, and at worst another disaster. When in any doubt at all, stick to your game plan!

Along this same general line, perhaps one additional way of losing yourself in a fog should be mentioned. That is the problem beginning writers sometimes have when they speak of how "My characters just took over the story and went their own way."

I hope you never heard yourself saying such a thing. Because did you ever stop to think how strange such a statement really is? How can your characters take over your story or anything else? *They are not real.* You made them up. They exist only in your head. And you are the author. You are the one in charge!

Part of your job as a creative writer is to control, discipline, and channel your imagination—not passively let it freewheel like a runaway truck. If it seems those characters *in your head* want to go a way other than the way you planned, either there's something wrong with your plot, and you're changing it in your subconscious, or . . .

If you get lost in the fog during the writing of a story, don't blame the characters! If you're lost, it's either because of a faulty concept at the start or loss of the conflict line. Characters can't do anything because they don't exist except as your imaginative constructs.

Characters taking over, new "inspirations" coming out of left field, and all the other good stuff amateurs imagine is a part of writing are all results of imperfect technique, laziness, poor planning, or lack of understanding of basic writing principles. They may look interesting in an old Rod Serling episode on late-night TV reruns, but they're just as nutty as everything else in "The Twilight Zone."

You are in control. It's your story. When things seem to go wrong, or you feel lost, careful analysis of your planning and the copy you've written to date, along with review of basic techniques, will show you what really has gone wrong. Then you can fix the problem.

There's nothing mysterious in the process. Always remember that.

26

Don't Worry About Being Obvious

STUDENT WRITERS OFTEN WORRY ABOUT BEING "TOO OBVIOUS." THEY SEEM to believe that they should be as subtle as possible in describing characters or defining story goals.

Nothing could be further from the truth, and professional writers know it. Every time you try to be subtle, you run the risk of losing your reader's understanding.

If you ever do happen to be too obvious in an otherwise excellent story, you can be sure that an alert editor somewhere down the line can trim a few words or phrases to make something less obvious. On the other hand, if you try to be subtle and the editor doesn't get the point, the story is going to be rejected.

There are three places where writers most fear being obvious: in defining a character; in stating a character's goal; and in pointing out the significance of a plot development. These are interrelated, but for purpose of discussion let's separate them and look, one at a time.

Fear of being "too obvious" in delineating story characters seems to be the main fear of inexperienced writers. They try to write about delicate shadings of action and motivation, and, in so doing, get so vague and willowy that the readers don't get the point at all. Sometimes, too, the misguided subtle writer would rather go to the gallows than slip in some direct comment—even by another character—about what kind of person the more major character is supposed to be. Usually the result is a fuzzy character.

Character portrayal is no place to be subtle. As pointed out in Chapter Seven, characters often are brought to life only by exaggeration. But in addition to this, characters can be made so subtle as to be lost entirely if the writer overindulges in delicate nuance . . . sly shifts of meaning. Consider using barnbrush strokes. Please. If you want the character to be bad, don't just have his lip curl, for heaven's sake! I the reader won't get it. Consider having Mr. Bad smoke nasty black cigars, forget to bathe, hate little children, and kick kitty-cats. I the reader may think you're crude, but I'll get the message.

And also try to jettison your fear of the obvious in terms of what you may want to say about the character. If you have a good handle on the character's dominant impression, go ahead and risk introducing him with a direct author statement, such as:

> James Marx was a mean man all his life, and no one had ever liked him. He never gave an inch in business, and he never gave a cent to charity. Of all who knew him, his wife liked him best; she merely detested him.

Crude? Sure. And of course the technique of direct author intrusion can easily be overdone. On the other hand, however, some mighty fine writers have been "guilty" of overt author intrusion no less blatant. Consider Sidney Sheldon. Consider Ernest Hemingway. Consider the greatest of them all, Charles Dickens. Is Ebenezer Scrooge *subtle*? Is Pip, in *Great Expectations*? Is Oliver Twist? Or consider Uriah Heep, one of Dicken's greatest creations. How many times does the wily, crafty, lying Mr. Heep speak of how "umble" he is, how "umble" is his family, how "umble" he feels about his job, while all the time slinking around, rubbing bony hands together, almost reptilian in his self-abasing scheme to take over the entire company?

Great characters come from the fertility and power of the author's imagination. But in addition to the power to imagine such characters, the writer must have the wit to know when to be blunt and obvious—and the courage to face down the fear of being "obvious."

A good exercise for a learning writer in this area is indulging in the gentle art of Frankenstein. Remember the monster? Hardly a subtle fellow.

What you might profit greatly from doing as an exercise is to play Dr. Frankenstein on your own. Sit down and try to create the greatest monster of exaggeration you can imagine. Allow nothing in this character portrayal to be subtle. Exaggerate everything. Spell out every aspect of personality. Leave nothing to the reader's imagination.

Then, having created, write a scene or two putting your monster of exaggeration into action. Have him or her talk, act, perform. Are you getting a picture as you write? Is it . . . just . . . barely . . . *possible* . . . that you're having fun with this? Is it conceivable that you're writing about a far more vivid and interesting character than you ever wrote about before?

Subtlety, thy name is doom!

But refusal to be obvious in drawing character is only one possible flaw. Another potentially fatal error of subtlety often centers on character *goal*. I have no idea why so many new writers cringe at the idea of overtly stating what it is a character *wants*. Such writers would rather have the character drift in, smile a lot, and sort of accidentally reveal his intentions on page 66. Or possibly allow some other character to guess. Or sigh a lot and say he doesn't want to talk about it.

Whether in a scene or in a planning sequel, your character should think about his goal, worry about his goal, talk about his goal, and try to get his goal. And you the writer have to keep reminding me the reader what it is, because if I forget for a moment, I won't understand the story any more!

It's no place to be subtle. Subtlety will confuse the reader about the meaning of plot actions, but in addition it will fuzz the reader's perception of what kind of character is being portrayed. For yea and verily, it hath often been said, but almost as often forgotten: "Tell me what a character wants, and I shall tell you who and what the character is."

Finally, don't make the mistake of trying to be subtle about what plot happenings mean—and don't ever downplay their significance! Readers confuse easily. If you have *any* doubt that the reader will understand the meaning of what someone in the story says or does, you must work in at once some method of pointing out what you may think is obvious. I mean, if the family's pioneer home burns to the ground on a bitter winter night, don't *assume* the reader will get it. And don't be subtle. Either directly say something like: "*Now the family faced death by exposure to the cold,*" or have one of the characters say something like, "*I'm really scared now. Without shelter we won't last through the day.*"

For some reason or other, as with other absolutely necessary comments which enter into every good story, many inexperienced writers are afraid to take the step. "The reader already *knows* that!" the poor author protests, or "I don't want to insult the reader's intelligence!" or "Wouldn't saying it clearly be sort of obvious?"

There is nothing wrong with "obvious" in these areas! Obvious is good. Obvious is mandatory. Obvious is next to cleanliness in the pantheon of fine qualities in fiction. Your story is *not* going to be pored over by textual detectives in the English Department at Stanford or Yale. Your reader is going to be careless, lazy, in a hurry, distracted, and none too patient when she reads your copy. She isn't going to get *anything* you don't put down there pretty clearly.

Well, at least do this much for me, just as a trial: put down all the obvious stuff in first draft. *Make sure there is no subtlety*. Then, if you insist, take it all out—"subtle it up" like crazy—on revision.

This way you'll at least have written the draft of a readable story.

Or, to be more positive, let's state the point this way: what seems obvious to the writer may be obscure as hell to the poor reader. And you're writing for the reader, not for yourself. Aren't you?

Check your copy. Ask yourself where you might have been carelessly or purposely subtle or unclear. Straighten it out. Make the point obvious! Drop your fears. If you're like almost all the learning writers I have ever known, being too obvious is the least of your problems. Being obscure—whether intentionally or by accident—may rank near the top of your woes.

My problem student, Wally, once brought me a scene in which his western hero was shot. The bullet hit the hero, knocking him down, and Wally then wrote:

> Bart looked down at the gaping hole in his chest, and realized

he was paralyzed from the neck down. He was bleeding to death.
He decided this was serious.

I told Wally I thought he might have overdone it.

But unless your story statement is in Wally's league of obviousness, don't worry about it. Anything short of the Wally standard is probably going to turn out just about right.

27

Don't Criticize Yourself to Death

ONE OF THE HARDEST THINGS A WRITER HAS TO DO IS TO LEARN HOW TO BE self-critical (which leads to improvement) but *not* picky, worrisome or fretful. For all those negative, self-doubting attitudes are self-destructive.

Sure, you should—you must—look at your copy with a critical eye, always trying to see flaws and problems that need improving. But you must be aware of the danger of going too far, of getting stale and scared and beginning to beat up on yourself rather than trying to help yourself improve.

The most common form of lethal self-criticism, it seems to me, is often heard in the young writer's wail, "This story I wrote is really dumb!" Or, "I hate my lead character; she's really dumb!" Or, "This whole plot line is dumb!"

What writers who utter such lines are really saying, I think, might be paraphrased as follows: "This is the best I can do, but I'm deathly afraid it isn't slick and clever enough, and therefore you are going to think I'm a stupid person for having written it."

Such fears are as much a part of writing fiction as headaches, wads of crumpled paper on the floor, and rejection slips. When you write fiction, whether you realize it or not (and at some level you probably do), you are risking revelation of your dreams and deepest emotions. It's frightening to reveal yourself this way, even indirectly. Further, the act of writing is tied very close to a person's ego structure; I have seen students shaky with worry when I was about to read one of their routine classroom essays, or even a brief paragraph of factual material. "*Criticize my work, criticize my personal essence*," the feeling seems to be. The most humdrum piece of writing somehow represents the writer's worth as a person sometimes. Small wonder, then, that the writer of a story or even (horrors!) a novel often gets worried sick—literally—about whether the reader may think it's dumb. Because if it's dumb, the writer is dumb. And if the writer is dumb, he is also, ipso facto, worthless, an object of potential ridicule . . . doomed.

Thus it's perfectly natural for you to worry that some character or bit of dialogue or plot line you just wrote may be "dumb."

It's natural—but it's also dangerous.

Especially when you're writing rough draft in a story, your job is *not* to be a critic. It's to be a creator. Any thought during this time that "This is dumb" is a *bad* thought, a thought likely to screw up the imaginative process. If such a thought comes to you as you're writing early-draft copy, you must recognize it as bad, toss it out of your mind, and simply press on.

As I'm sure you know, the human brain is composed of two hemispheres. The right hemisphere, or half, is the seat of emotion, imagination, creativity and intuition. The left hemisphere is the logical side, the analyzer, language processor, critic. The two halves of the brain communicate with one another, but imperfectly; there is even one theory that says much of psychological theory is really the result of the left hemisphere's attempts to make sense of stuff felt and done by the right side, which is impulsive and basically kind of crazy, and essentially unexplainable!

Given this bicameral brain of yours, consider what goes on when you write. Ideas, pictures, characters and plots drift out of the right hemisphere. They have no shape and no linearity. So you turn on your left side and analyze, logicalize, form, *plan*. Then you sit down to write your first draft, which is to say, to dream a patterned dream; and the right hemisphere is called on to do that.

The left hemisphere, however, is not entirely decommissioned while the first-draft dreaming is going on. The left has to process the language, and it has to stand by in the wings, watching the performance, auditing it to make sure that the dream doesn't suddenly lose all form and direction. Then, later, during revisions, the left-side critic may come much more to the fore, seeing logical problems, examining story pattern, character motives, the purity of the grammar and spelling, and so on.

So writing fiction becomes a most strange and wonderful product of an alliance between the hemispheres of your brain, in which first one, then the other, hemisphere is dominant.

Note: during the dream stage of the writing, as you are actually producing copy, it is the creative right hemisphere that is in charge, with the left-side critic only passively watching most of the time. But any thought such as "*This is dumb*!" or "*People are going to think this scene is dumb*!" are obviously messages from the left side of the brain—critical messages that you don't need at this time, while the right side is rolling.

To put this another way, I think most "this is dumb" fear messages are destructive for two reasons: 1. They get the wrong side of the brain in charge and thwart the creative process, and 2. They signal a revolt inside your head that can only lead to fear and further slowing of your story's progress.

There is a time for the left-side critic. But during the writing of a draft is not that time. You use your left side to make your plans, draw your outlines, lay out your characters. But once you start down the creative highway of writing a draft, you keep that logical roadmap on the seat beside you; *you don't keep reading it while you're driving*.

Once you have made your plans and started writing, it's part of your writer's discipline to recognize the negative, destructive nature of all "this is dumb" fears. We all have our writing tied closely to our ego, and we're all scared. But we can't let the fear slow us down, and we can't let that old villainous left-hemisphere critic mess things up. Once under way, you have to trust yourself—that partly logical creative roadmap of an outline or synopsis you planned earlier—and follow it with enthusiasm and imagination and joy.

At this point I can almost hear you the reader of these words wailing, "But sometimes what I write really *is* dumb!"

Well, sure. Even Shakespeare wrote some dumb stuff. So what? If you write something really dumb, the world isn't going to end. And please note: if you're writing, your first job is to press on and follow the imagination, located in your right hemisphere. If what you're putting down is really dumb, you can fix it later, during revision.

How will you know later if it's really dumb? Sometimes you can never be entirely sure and have to make an arbitrary decision, almost a coin toss—"It really is dumb, so I'll change it," or "I don't think it really is dumb, so I'll leave it alone." Most of the time, however, if you write through the original yammering of the left-side critic, when you come back to the questioned segment later you will have a clearer head and see at once whether it really is dumb or not. It's the impulsive fear during creation that's seldom if ever clear and accurate.

Plan . . . write . . . then fix. Keep the phases separate as much as possible. And don't beat up on yourself during any phase.

Recognize this: part of growing up as a fiction writer is the ultimate recognition that *all* of us are scared: of looking dumb, of running out of ideas, of never selling our copy, of not getting noticed. We fiction writers make a business of being scared, and not just of looking dumb. Some of these fears may never go away, and we may just have to learn to live with them. The fear of looking dumb, though, can be tossed away once you've recognized it as the jealous yammering of a left hemisphere critic who's tired of being forced to sit silent in the corner while the right side plays.

You'll still get the thought that it's dumb, sometimes. And you'll still be scared, worried about embarrassment. But maybe now you see that the only really dumb thing is to think it's dumb.

Finally, look at the other side of the question. Your plight could be infinitely worse. You could be one of that small, truly doomed minority who thinks every word they write is precious, every idea immortal, every character a demigod, every plot a classic. They *never* think anything they write is dumb. So they never self-criticize even at the times they should, never listen to advice, never study published writers, and spend all their emotional energy defending the rocky turf of their enormous ego. You know the type I mean; you undoubtedly know one of them. Mention a problem you see in one of their stories and they say you just don't understand.

Suggest changing so much as a punctuation mark on their page and they go crazy: "*I* don't change my copy! *My* copy is perfect! To change a word of *this*" (slapping the page with the back of her hand) "would be a violation of my artistic inspiration and integrity!!!"

These are the folks who really should be worrying, because if they won't listen and be open, they can't grow. And if they can't grow, they've had it.

So maybe you now see why your worries about "being dumb" aren't nearly as bad as other things that could be messing you up. All you've got to do, after all, is *stop it.*

So stop it.

28

Don't Worry What Mother Will Think

IN THE LAST CHAPTER WE POINTED OUT HOW UNHEALTHY FRIGHTENED SELF-criticism can be for the fiction writer. Closely related to this kind of worried hang-up is concern about what other people might think of the writer once her story is published.

Usually the feared future critic is mother. Sometimes it's a husband or wife, a child, or even a dear friend. (I spent some time during the early years of my writing career worrying what a sainted aunt would think.)

Such worries are normal, but you must not let them hamstring your creative efforts. If you can't entirely banish such worry from your mind, then consider adopting a pen name. For you have plenty of other things to worry about, and frightened self-censorship simply has to be jettisoned at once.

Of course you want to be bound by the dictates of good sense and good taste. But these are a far cry from groundless worries about a stern and unforgiving moral arbiter. One of the great joys of writing fiction is that you are *free*. You must believe this and act like it. You must never, ever allow yourself to get hung up on fears of what some family member or friend might think on a personal level.

29

Don't Hide From Your Feelings

CLOSELY RELATED TO FRIGHTENED SELF-CRITICISM AND WORRY ABOUT FAMily or friends is a more subtle fear that some writers carry to their work without ever realizing it. That is the fear of strong emotional feelings. I have met several enormously talented students who never sold their stories because their copy was devoid of real emotion; these writers feared strong feelings in real life and simply couldn't face such feelings in their writing.

If you want to succeed as a writer of fiction, you must never hide from your own feelings because they provide for you your most essential contact with your story characters—and potential readers.

Now, in real life many of us were brought up to distrust or even ignore our innermost emotions. Our "training" as children or young adults may even have been so strenuous in this regard that we do not recognize the self-censorship.

Do you recognize any such distrust or blocking of emotions within yourself? Perhaps as a small child you gave in (quite naturally) to infant feelings of fear and abandonment; perhaps you had all sorts of problems coming to terms with your baby-impulses to have what you wanted or needed, *now*, and a growing and unpleasant awareness that Mother or Dad suddenly expected you to "behave," "be patient," or "be responsible." Maybe you had a temper tantrum and were punished; or you cried in frustration of your wishes and were studiously ignored; or you yielded to some vengeful impulse and were severely scolded (and therefore scared all the more).

It's a ghastly process, when you stop to think about it, this business of growing out of infanthood into childhood . . . the later process of "acting your age," "being a good soldier," etc. You're *little*. You're *helpless*. You're *scared*. If Mother doesn't attend to you instantly, your fear rises that she won't help you at all; and without her you're *dead*. At a very young age you resent this, and want to be on your own; but you can't be, yet, and even if it were physically possible, all sorts of psychological drives push you desperately toward reunion with Mom at the same time a little bit of you . . . maybe . . . resents and even hates her.

Many of these primitive feelings are unacceptable. We know it at a very early age, and God knows our parents start telling us about it very soon. So we are torn, and our very survival seems to depend on our "doing better." We learn to do better either by hiding what we're feeling, or denying—even to ourselves—that such unacceptable feelings are inside us.

These same mechanisms are reinforced later, in school and with friends and associates. We continue to learn about our feelings, and unfortunately a lot of the lessons in life tend to tell us: *Be cool. Don't feel that way.*

But if you do feel that way, don't show it.

And so sometimes we really and truly block out many emotions—perhaps blocking out some "good" ones with all the seemingly "bad" ones—and perhaps we become "adult" by really and truly not feeling anything at all very much anymore.

Or we still feel . . . some . . . but hide it from everyone else, and feel guilty and try to deny even to ourselves.

It may be that you are one of the lucky ones, in touch with your feelings in all their ranges, and capable of expressing such emotions in a healthy way at least part of the time. Even if you are one of these, however, I suspect that when it comes to your fiction writing, you may have an impulse to "cool it" somewhat in dread of looking odd to your reader, or "dumb," or "too sentimental."

We still live in an age that looks askance at direct confrontation with many feelings, especially elemental ones such as rage and fright. But you as a writer of fiction must never hide from such feelings because they are absolutely essential to good stories.

You must observe yourself . . . your innermost, secret workings . . . and consider your feelings, working always to be more aware of them. Remember: You do not have to *act on* whatever feelings are there; but the more clearly you are aware of them in all their nuances, the better you can know and understand yourself.

You must observe others around you, using your references in your own emotions to try constantly to understand what they must be feeling emotionally, what primitive fires must be goading them.

And you must confront such feelings in your stories. Fiction characters who only *think* are dead. It is in their feelings that the readers will understand them . . . sympathize with them . . . care about their plight in the outcome of your fiction.

William Foster-Harris, a wise writing teacher who preceded me at the University of Oklahoma, used to talk endlessly about the necessity for a subjective view of reality if one were to write decent fiction. Foster-Harris, like a good parent, seems to me to grow in wisdom with each year I grow older. Strong emotion—so often ducked or ignored in real life—must be at the center of your stories.

The first roadblock, of course, is that you may not know your own feelings very well. I have known young writers who had to spend a brief time with a professional counselor or therapist to overcome this kind of blockage. However, such a step usually is not necessary. For you, it will probably be enough to make a strenuous attempt, in your private journal, to write down an honest and blunt description of your emotional state every day. Additionally, you may try to write brief descriptions of the exact emotional state you observe in some other person—or imagine in your character.

When you write, you may not write so overtly about the feelings . . . or sometimes you may. You might develop ways to show the physical effects of strong emotion—tears, a palsied hand, or clenched fist—and so define the imagined emotions indirectly, through the presented evidence. But in any case you cannot write fiction without being aware of the feelings inherent in your story people—and then having the courage to put them down on paper in some form.

In first draft, I think you would be wise to avoid any chance that you might still duck confrontation with powerful feelings. In other words, I would much prefer to see you write "too much" of feeling in your first draft; you can always tone it down a bit later, after sober reflection, if such trimming really seems to be called for. On the other hand, a sterile, chill, emotionless story, filled with robot *people* will never be accepted by any reader.

One more word on this topic: whether defining a character's inner life or planning a powerful and harrowing scene in your story, you should avoid the impulse to "play safe." The world's greatest literature has been produced about people on the edge—by writers with the gumption to walk on an edge of their own, on the precipice of sentimentality, melodrama, or some other literary excess. "Better safe than sorry," goes the old warning. But in fiction it just doesn't work. "Safe" will *always* be sorry for the writer dealing with character emotions and strong plot situations.

Face feelings. Then take the risk! Walk on the very edge of some situation or scene that will be *horrible* if you write one word too much . . . carry it one step too far. For it's only on the brink of the abyss where great fiction is written. And nobody ever really had too much fun playing it safe all the time, did they?

30

Don't Take It to the Club Meeting

USUALLY IT'S A MISTAKE TO SEEK ADVICE FROM OTHER AMATEURS AT WRITERS' clubs. I don't think it's a good idea to ask family or friends to read and "criticize" your manuscript, either.

If you want to share your work with your spouse or a close friend, that's fine. But to ask a club member, relative or friend for criticism is mostly a waste of time for at least two reasons: they won't be honest; they usually don't know what they're doing anyway.

Of course your writer's club may have a much-published professional as a member. If you can get advice from that person, it might be a fine thing. But most writers' clubs are filled almost entirely with unpublished writers, or those whose minor newspaper credits don't qualify them to judge your copy.

I have nothing against clubs of writers. I belong to a couple myself and sometimes attend meetings. They provide companionship, a place to meet others involved in the same kind of fascinating work, sometimes sources of market and other information, and new friends.

Far too many of them, however, encourage members to read their copy aloud for group dissection and discussion. This is *always* a waste of time. Reading your copy aloud is not the normal "delivery system" for a story. It's written to be read in print, not read aloud by the author.

Also, whether you read your copy aloud to club members or circulate copies to them, your club audience is in no way a normal audience of the kind you want to please. There are people here who have failed and are bitter. There are others here to show off. There are others who are here for a chance to pontificate. There are know-it-alls and know-nothings. If your work is good, many of them will be jealous. If your work is bad, few, if any, of them will know how to point out your mistakes in a constructive manner.

There are not likely to be any honest critical responses to your work. Club members generally try to be as gentle and positive as family members. A few, perhaps in reaction, crucify every member. In neither case do you get anything like an objective reaction.

Further, to be blunt about it, most writing club members have no idea what makes a good story. There's no conceivable way they can give you more than a groping, subjective reaction.

Remember, too, that many such club members get competitive and want to "shine" during the discussion period. They may say *anything* just so they can get on their feet and have their moment in the spotlight.

Finally, it has been my observation that no two writer's club "experts"—i.e., regular critics who seldom if ever publish anything of their own—ever agree on anything about writing. So if more than one advises you, you're going to get conflicting advice that's only more confusing than none at all.

The following is an amalgam of reports I've heard from students who took work to a writer's club. I can't say that any single person had all of these things happen to them, but I've known a couple of writers who took work to several meetings in succession and *almost* went through the full list that follows:

At the first meeting, somebody sniggered while she read her copy.

At the second, someone else cried while she read other pages.

At the third, the vice president said the ending of the story reminded her of Chekov; she pronounced it "great"

At the fourth meeting, after studying the revised story, someone suggested sharply trimming the dialogue; someone else stood up and said the story needed *more* dialogue.

At the fifth meeting—well, perhaps you get the idea.

And so it goes. Writers' clubs are fine organizations for many reasons, and sometimes they bring in professionals for lectures, which can be helpful. But as dearly as I love these clubs, and as many needs as I can see they fill for members, my advice remains the same: don't read for them; you'll get nothing out of it, and you might end up more confused.

The writing competitions often sponsored by writing clubs or coalitions, often in conjunction with annual conferences, are also dangerous for the serious writer, in my jaundiced opinion.

You know how these work. Three judges are (secretly) recruited for various contest categories such as short story, novel, chapter and so on. You prepare your entry pages with no hint of your identity, and an official removes your identifying entry form, codes it and your manuscript with a matching ID number, and then passes your entry along to the judges, who read, rank, and comment in turn. After the smoke clears, you may win a first, second or third prize, or honorable mention, in your category. There may be a small cash prize involved. Even if you don't win, you at least get back the written comments of the judges.

Presumably these comments help you improve your work.

Maybe sometimes they do. But in my experience, which is not narrow, the comments and advice from judges can vary as widely—and wildly—as comments from the club meeting floor after a reading. One judge will tell you to build up your scenes, and the next will tell you to cut them. One will praise your descriptive passages, and the next will suggest cutting them. One will wax poetic about how wonderful your plot is, and the next may say she couldn't find a plot at all.

In earlier and more innocent years I helped judge a number of fiction contests myself. Like all judges, I put an incredible amount of time into the job, and tried my level best to be both critical and helpful. But there is a nasty little secret about writing anonymous comments and suggestions to an anonymous writer out there somewhere: *In most cases, the advice cannot possibly fix the problem.*

Why should that be so? Because problems in writing fiction—tactics, planning, plotting, characterization, structure and the like—all tie together in the finished product. For example, a harrowing scene simply cannot be written about a dull and unrealized character. Sparkling dialogue may be written, but it means nothing if it does not somehow advance the plot. Plot cannot be discussed without some discussion of building backstory, and probably hidden story as well. Everything relates to everything else. Style is a subject requiring a course by itself for its proper examination.

Now consider the judge. Most novels he will look at during the average contest have quite a lot wrong with them. The problems interrelate. As much as he may like some fragments of the manuscript, chances are it would take him 25,000 words to begin to outline everything he sees wrong.

There are two major problems with this. First, he doesn't have time to write 25,000 words. Second, if he did, the resulting critique would probably seem so cruel and destructive to the writer that harm would be done to her.

Therefore, the judge scrawls a few paragraphs that he *hopes* may be in the critical ballpark, and even help. But it's a weak, limping attempt, and always falls short. And without face-to-face discussion, even the best advice may be misunderstood.

Strangely, however, some writers desperate for *any* recognition can sometimes get hooked on contests. Tragically, they start substituting contest recognition for real-world commercial sales. Contests and readings are nice amateur activities. For some writers they represent the ultimate, and there's nothing wrong with that. But I assume your goals are more ambitious—the national, paid markets. In that case, any satisfaction you might get from a club contest showing would only threaten to lower the fire in your belly—your resolve to show your work in the only place it really matters, the professional marketplace.

Join and attend meetings of a writer's club if you wish, by all means. But leave your story home.

Believe me. At some point, when you have broken into the professional ranks, you will start getting advice of a far different sort: the advice of an editor who knows what she is doing—and who has a checkbook in her hand.

That's when you listen most attentively.

31 Don't Ignore Professional Advice

IN THE PREVIOUS CHAPTER WE WARNED AGAINST TAKING TOO MUCH ADVICE from fellow amateurs, and noted that one day you may get lucky enough to have an editor fall in love with your work and give you sound guidance. There is also another possible source of good, face-to-face advice on your own work, and that's study with a published author who also knows how to teach his craft.

If you can find a professional who knows how to teach the craft of fiction, you should, therefore, go out of your way to work with her. And if that teaching pro gives you advice, you should not ignore it; you should at least consider it most seriously, and even try it, even if only for a short, experimental period.

Having said this, I hasten to add a number of provisos.

First, it *is* possible to learn how to write by writing, studying models, and reading books and articles about the craft. At least as far back as the early part of this century, seasoned professional writers were producing books containing technical advice that are just as solid today as when they were written. Only a few weeks before writing these words, I read a magazine article that repeated some of that old material and saw that it was still sound. And in the same issue of the same magazine I came upon a brief piece that said something about the introduction of characters that I had never before seen stated so clearly or meaningfully.

So it's possible.

There are, however, some problems with trying to learn only from books, with no professional coaching.

One obvious problem is that no book can give you a specific drill or test to make absolutely certain you understand a point; it can't read your copy, discuss it with you, hammer away at the same point until it is sure you understand and are applying a given technique. Books and articles, to say it another way, can't give you the individual feedback and coaching of a real teacher.

Another problem is that books on the techniques of writing usually cover many aspects of the craft, just as this one does. If you are struggling to learn, *it may be that you don't know what you most need to work on*. You might read right past a passage or section that might make all the difference for you if it were stressed for you and emphasized by someone who could see the flaw in your copy. In other words, the single vital point for *your* work might get lost in the panoply of suggestions you read through.

(That, incidentally, is one reason why this book is set up in a series of short "don't" episodes; the hope is that you have some idea of where your problems may lie, and will, after reading through everything, return to specific sections that you consider problem areas for *you*, giving them additional consideration and study.)

In addition, books and articles can't set deadlines for you. Now, I know you are highly motivated, or you wouldn't be reading *this* book. But all of us tend to procrastinate. And no matter how much I might try in these pages, I simply can't put the kind of work pressure on you that I could if you were one of my class students, scheduled to bring in pages each week . . . or face both my wrath and a failing grade.

Finally, no book or article can encourage you when you feel low, beat up on you when you're being lazy, pick out a good passage and praise it, or point out the error in another page of your copy. A good writing coach is not just a teacher; he is advisor, handholder, slave driver, critic, friend, psychologist, editor, even inspirational guru.

So by all means study books on writing. Sift the advice, compare what different authors may say, and work to find your own way. But in addition, if you can, find a professional writing teacher, *listen to what she says*, and then *try to do it*.

Having said this with such certainty, however, I must add that there are all sorts of perils inherent in this seemingly harmless advice. We should consider a few of them.

First, a great number of fine fiction writers have no idea—or *say* they have no idea—of how they get the job done. Personally I believe that some may actually work by unconscious imitation, trial and error, and a genius-imagination, and truly not have any clear idea of how they are writing good stories. Unfortunately—again personal opinion—I think a far greater number of professional writers who profess to be mystified by the creative process are putting on an act for the public. "It makes me look more mysterious and wonderful if I act like it's all inspiration," they seem to be thinking. Or, "If people realized that I'm practicing a craft, they would think less of me."

(Such attitudes don't come only from writers who want to be mysterious and mystical to the general public; such attitudes are, unfortunately, endemic in college English departments, where instructors of literature seldom understand anything about the way writers really work, and so stress the mystery angle in order to allow the existence of little journals and magazines where abstruse theories of the most outrageous kind can be published . . . and shown to other faculty members who vote on matters of tenure and promotion. For this reason, English literature teachers seldom make good writing coaches, for the same reason that football fans seldom make good players or coaches; you can't learn the game from the bleachers, and you can't learn what writing is really all about from the theoretical ivory tower, either.)

But back to real writers who say they don't know what they're doing when they do it—or can't talk about their craft in a way that's meaningful for others: a few, neither ignorant of their craft nor wanting to look mysterious, are simply too lazy to think their way logically through the patterns of their own work. Or maybe they're scared that if they think about it, it will go away.

By this time, not so incidentally, I imagine you must be wondering why I've gone to such lengths talking about writers and teachers who *can't do it*, when in fact the subject of this chapter is advice that you should find a pro and listen to her. It's precisely because of the existence out there of so many teachers who can't teach, for whatever reason. I've talked about the bad ones to emphasize to you that I'm saying you should get help from a pro, and do what's advised, *only when you locate a good teacher-professional.*

How can you tell if the local guru is for real? You launch a polite investigation.

Ask people about her. Get some idea of her reputation generally. Then write or telephone the teacher-pro and try to set up an appointment to discuss possible coaching. If the pro is agreeable, and preliminary talk about times and costs are acceptable, then you see the teacher in person, ask a few questions, and size her up one-to-one.

Watch out for statements like the following:

"Well, it's all very mysterious, actually. . . ."

"I believe in giving my student total freedom. . . ."

"Sometimes I feel I learn more from my students than they can possibly learn from me. . . ."

"I will never *tell* you to do or try anything. . . ."

"As William Faulkner once said. . . ."

"As Henry James once wrote. . . ."

"In the words of the immortal Ezra Pound. . . ."

And all such stuff that says 1. The teacher isn't going to teach, and 2. What we're really going to be into here is a disguised literature appreciation course.

If the teacher seems to pass the preliminary test, your second step should be to ask her for a list of successful students. She should be able to provide the names of some former students who are now selling copy. You should also get the names of a few present or very recent students. You should call up some of these people and discuss the teacher with them, finding out what their opinion is, what they feel they are accomplishing.

Finally, if all is well so far, you should submit a piece of copy to the teacher and see what kind of a critique and advice you get. If it seems airy and highfalutin, I think you should run. If it seems basic, pragmatic and practical—even if you don't agree with all of it—then maybe you have found your pro.

But let's assume now that you've gotten lucky, and you are working with someone who produces professional copy herself, and seems to be giving you hard-nosed, practical advice. Now you must *do what you're told.*

This is harder than it sounds for at least three reasons:

First, as we said before in this book, writing is tied painfully close to your ego; suggestions for basic changes in your approach to writing may be psychologically so uncomfortable that you make up all kinds of excuses not to listen.

Second, most new things are a little painful. Your most basic impulse, when told to try something new, will be not to like it—resist trying it.

Third, you may be so in love with your present way of writing—even though you aren't selling with it—that you just get angry and dig your heels in when told to do it some other way.

And most insidious of all—*you actually may not be able to hear what the teacher is really saying.* This is a tough one, and I don't know what you can do about it beyond remembering that it's a pretty common phenomenon. Even in a nutshell the problem is complex, but here it is, as simply as I can state it:

If you don't know what you don't know, then there's no way for you to hear advice designed to remedy the problem.

When I was first starting out with a professional teacher—after more than seven years of trying to make it on my own—he promptly began telling me to do a certain thing in setting up the major scenes in my novels. Week after week, month after month, year after year, he told me exactly the same thing. I kept imagining I understood what he was saying. My copy remained directionless—flabby.

Finally, after a woefully long time, I realized on my own something like, "*Hey, I need better scene-endings that will further trap the hero.*"

Only then, having realized that I didn't know how to do this, was I able to walk into my teacher's office the very next week and *finally hear him telling me what I now saw I needed to know*—as he had been doing all along.

This is a point that's hard for people to understand if they have never experienced it. But it's very common for me to have a student walk up to me after a given session and say, in effect, "Why in the world didn't you ever tell me that before?" And almost always I can then take him back to lecture notes from previous courses, and even personal critiques written earlier to him about his copy, which said exactly what he was never ready to take in and apply before.

That's why I so emphasize that, if you find a competent teaching pro, you must really, really listen . . . strenuously struggle to hear what is actually being said . . . then work your hardest to do *exactly* as you're told.

It may be that you'll find in the long run that some given bit of advice just doesn't work for you. That's okay. But if you reject advice out of hand, and never try it, then you can never really know, can you?

There are things about the workings of the imagination and the creative process that are indeed mysterious. But most of the craft of writing *can* be taught, and it can be learned.

All it takes is someone who knows what he's doing, at one end of the dialogue, and someone who is truly willing to listen and try, at the other.

32

Don't Chase the Market

AS A PROFESSIONAL WRITER OF FICTION, YOU CAN GO CRAZY TRYING TO OUT-guess the editors . . . trying to figure out where the market might go next, or just what such and such publisher "must *really* want." You can waste far too much emotional energy trying to get out in front of the latest trend.

Having said that, let me quickly add that you must, of course, do everything in your power to keep abreast of trends in the sales of fiction. If you're working in the shorter lengths, you should maintain close touch with each new marketing aid such as *Writer's Market* and/or *Literary Marketplace*. Magazines change their emphasis from time to time, sometimes in response to new orders from a publisher seeking out a new readership audience, sometimes because a new editor comes in with new and different ideas. These changes will be reflected in published statements about what the magazine wants . . . eventually. So at least you should check in with your local library or bookstore every so often to find market aids.

In addition, it goes without saying (doesn't it?) that you should read and study your target magazines on a continuing basis. A new editor might alter the magazine's desires today, and it could be more than a year before any library/book marketing publication reflected the change. If you are alert and analytical in your magazine reading, you'll spot the new emphasis far sooner.

Magazines for writers are a gold mine of up-to-date market information. The "how-to articles" will help; but you should not overlook the trade news section in the back of the magazine. This may provide your first hint that the times, they are a 'changin' at your target publication.

For the novelist, a study of the publisher's latest fiction list may provide valuable clues. Ask your local newspaper book reviewer or bookstore owner to share the publishers' catalogues with you. You can see what kind of novels this publisher is publishing—the catalogue will provide an illustration and plot summary, both of which can be helpful. The *ranking* of books to be printed in the near future may provide you with valuable clues, too: it's easy to pick out, from wealth of illustration, space and placement in the catalogue which novels are that publisher's expected "leaders" in the next quarter.

Finally, some publishers (especially the romance publishers) can provide you with sometimes-elaborate "tip sheets" that specify all sorts of things that publisher wants or doesn't want in submitted novels. It's common for such tip sheets to tell you the desired age of the central characters, settings that the editors may be overstocked on, etc. A letter of enquiry together with a stamped, self-addressed envelope (SASE), will bring you the tip sheets.

All of these aids keep you from writing a good book that is simply not acceptable because of publisher prejudices you might have learned about at the outset. All such aids and studies help you learn more as a novelist.

On the other hand—and hence the title of this chapter—it's a common observation among publishing professionals that too many new novelists hang themselves up trying to find "a sure thing" in publishing. Chances are that even the tip sheet you get from a publisher today will include no-no's that you might include in a novel and still sell to that publisher, if everything else about the book was wonderful. There just are not a lot of ironclad rules at book length.

Further, trends change with astonishing speed in book publishing today. By the time you got a tip sheet saying submarine stories were "in"—and Tom Clancy's best-seller was being made into a movie—a dozen other publishers might have jumped on the bandwagon to prepare submarine novels of their own, glutting the market *and ending the trend*. Not long ago, spy novels involving the CIA and the KGB were hot stuff. Then the Soviet Union changed drastically . . . readers grew tired of such spy maneuvers . . . and the subgenre died on the vine.

Maybe you can spot a developing hot trend and get your book written in time. But it's chancy business. Even if you guess perfectly, a lot of other people are probably guessing right along with you. And then it's going to take you a year to write this hot idea . . . a year to sell it . . . another year to get it through the editing and publishing process.

And how hot is that hot trend really going to be in three years?

For all these reasons, chasing after the market can be a self-defeating process. In addition, consider how much creative, analytical energy market-chasers expend, trying to outfox the trendsetters. Might it not be more profitable to stay aware of trends generally, yet concentrate your energies on simply *writing the best novel you know how to write*?

In today's crazy fiction markets, it's devilishly difficult to outguess the future. You may hear people say they have it figured out. Don't let them make you uneasy. Your business is creating stories. If you do that well enough, the trends will tend to take care of themselves.

Be aware. Pay attention to the business end of writing. But always keep in the back of your mind a reassuring fact: every hot new fiction trend was started by a lonely writer, working alone, bucking whatever the last trend seemed to be, and creating such a grand story that it started a new trend the moment it was published.

Or to put that another way: the best books don't follow trends; they establish them.

33

Don't Pose and Posture

YOUR STYLE AND ATTITUDE IN YOUR STORIES SHOULD BE LIKE A CLEAN PANE of glass through which the reader sees the action. If you pose and posture in your copy, you'll draw attention to you as a writer, rather than to what's happening on your page. And that's always bad.

The two kinds of posing and posturing that seem most widespread these days are:

- The Frustrated Poet
- The Tough Guy/Gal

Both are phony. Both may be sick. Both wreck fiction.

To make sure you won't do either of these acts, let's look briefly at each of them.

The frustrated poet act most often shows up when the writer is trying to do one of two good things: face a strong emotion in a character, or describe a striking bit of scenery. The writer usually decides to gear up and mount a massive effort to string together some really striking word-pictures. What results is what we sometimes call *a purple patch*—a few sentences or paragraphs crammed with adjectives and other crutch-words designed to "be pretty" or provide some "fine writing." At best it's a pretty but cumbersome and distracting effort to get at the finest detail, when presentation of such poetic detail isn't necessary for the reader's understanding of the story. At worst, the purple patch is the result of the writer's compulsion to show off the style that won her accolades from her sixth-grade English teacher.

The prototypical purple patch, mentioned once before in this book, is the "rosy fingers of dawn" chapter or scene opening. Such openings go something like this:

> As the rosy fingers of dawn painted gossamer strands of drifting cumulus over the vast and lovely expanse of the cyan night, a gentle zephyr nudged sleeping emerald leaves to sibilant stirrings, turning each tiny protoplasmic elf into a whispering, pirouetting dancer, intent upon welcoming the dawn of another warm and beautiful morning.

Such stuff when carried to the extreme shown in the example is obviously hilarious because the reader can almost see the poor writer sitting there at the keyboard, risking creative hernia and mounting tiny droplets of blood on her forehead. But even if the poetic effort isn't quite this absurd, it is still bad—and not only because it calls attention to the prose itself, rather than to the story. It's also destructive to the story because a story's momentum, for the reader, comes from the plot's forward movement. And when you stop to describe something, you have *stopped*. Thus, after such a passage, your job as a storyteller has been made harder because your first task becomes one of *getting things moving again*, off dead center.

Any time you find yourself sighing over a paragraph you have written, you are well advised to take a long, hard, more critical look at it. Ask yourself:

- Did this passage develop naturally? (Or did I force it?)
- Does this passage really contribute to necessary mood and tone? (Or did I stick it in to indulge myself?)
- Does this passage advance the story?
- Is there a simpler and more direct way to convey the same information?
- Am I storytelling here? (Or am I showing off?)

All of us have written passages we look back on with fondness. But the dead-stop poetic description will never be among them. Purple patches, signs of a frustrated poet rearing his shaggy head, may occur in first draft of a story as we let our imagination run, but on revision we must look hard at all such passages with an eye toward simplifying and cleaning up our act.

The tough guy/gal act also represents a false pose. In this case, the writer runs to the opposite end of the writing spectrum and *denies* all impulse at the delicate or the soft by being over-tough, over-cynical, over-gruff, or over-bitter.

I'll spare you an example of this kind of writing. You have seen too many examples in print, I suspect. Such writers tend to write about rough, tough heroes who grunt and curse and bash a lot.

In recent times, however, the male crusher-basher tough guy has a serious competitor: the tough-talking, neurotically independent "modern female." These women need no one, and talk and act as bad as their fictional male counterparts.

The existence of all such tough-talk fiction proves that a lot of authors are posing behind the act of creation.

It's crucial that you be yourself as an author, and not pose. Just to be sure, you might consider asking yourself the following question:

Am I acting tough in order to hide my true feelings behind the act?

If the answer is "yes," then you're operating a charade rather than writing honest fiction, and you ought to rethink things.

You see, the bottom line here is that you have only one thing that's yours and yours alone—only one unique item you can sell: yourself. Posing, whether it's as a sachet-sniffing poet or brass-knuckled bully, is still posing—may still represent flight from your own feelings, which are your most precious salable commodity. Ultimately, posturing is a symptom of fear. It's always self-defeating.

34

Don't Waste Your Plot Ideas

THIS SECTION IS AIMED PRIMARILY AT NOVELISTS.

If you've never written a book-length story before, one of the many interesting (and possibly dismaying) things you'll learn during construction of the first draft is simply how many incidents and events you have to dream up in order to "make length." It's possible to write a one-idea short story. But even the shortest novel contains dozens of plot ideas, subplots, minor incidents, and significant events.

One of your first creative jobs as a novelist, therefore, is to dream up enough stuff—a sufficient number of things to happen.

Very often, however, dreaming up the events proves to be relatively easy when compared with another related task, which is to make maximum use of plot developments once you've introduced them. Failure to make maximum use of plot ideas can make your job twice as hard, and possibly doom your novel, turning it into an illogical farrago of events rather than a continuous, interesting narrative.

Here's what I mean.

The amateur, unpublished novelist may insert a scene early in her book in which the hero meets a doorman at a hotel, gets some information from him, and walks away to act on that information. The doorman may be an interesting minor character, but he will never—as the amateur novelist tends to see it—enter the story again.

"Why did you put the doorman in the story?" I may ask.

Says Amateur Novelist: "To give the hero that info."

"Okay," I persist. "Now that you have the doorman in the book, what else can you invent that would involve him? *How else can you use what you've already made up*?"

Amateur Novelist (usually!): "Huh?"

Or suppose you've just imagined and written a scene in which your heroine has had a minor collision with another car, driven by the hero-to-be. You put in the accident so the two could meet. Fine. But again a professional coach will ask you, "What else can you make of that accident? *Can you think of other ways you can use it later in the story*?"

In the case of the doorman, he might be brought back into the story as a source of later information; he might turn out to know more than the hero so far got out of him—in which case all sorts of interesting questions immediately appear: "Why did he withhold information?" "What else does he know?" "How does he know it?" "How is the hero going to come to suspect that he held something back?" And so on.

In the case of the fender bender, plotted to make heroine meet hero, the professional will immediately begin to ponder questions such as the following, all under the general heading of *What other use can I make of the wreck?*:

- Did either party sustain an injury that might show up only later?
- Did someone see this accident and do something as a result?
- Can there be a lawsuit?
- What if the heroine's insurance fails to pay, and she has to sue the hero?
- What if her car later fails on a remote road because of hidden damage?
- Could he later joke about the wreck and "silly woman drivers," causing a furious argument?
- Can she later be preoccupied in some way about the wreck, causing her to forget something else?
- Is it possible that, as a result of the wreck, he—

You get the idea, I'm sure.

Professional novelists recognize that it's sometimes a problem, coming up with enough events and incidents in the first place. For that reason, they always think as in the example above, looking for ways to make maximum use of everything they invent. The grand by-product of such thinking is that more and more characters and events take on significance; various scenes and plot lines begin to link more tightly together, making the novel tighter, and more logical; and the reader tends to read with more attention and pleasure because *every page* is sure to be important not only for itself but in terms of later development.

Another minor but sometimes nagging problem for the novelist can also be solved by constant attention to maximum use of your material. That has to do with the way minor characters tend to proliferate in beginner copy. It's not unusual for the fledgling novelist to introduce that doorman in chapter one, a cabdriver in chapter two, a TV reporter and a yard person in chapter three—and a dozen more bit players by halfway through the book. But the simplest novel is complex enough, and nobody (neither the writer nor the reader!) wants to need a printed program to keep track of all the minor parts.

In such circumstances, you may solve some of your "cast of thousands" problems by being alert to how you may be able to use one character to handle several minor missions. For example, is it possible that that doorman could take over the work you assigned to the cabdriver and the yard man? Could the TV reporter from chapter three also provide the information you gave to the policeman in chapter seven—and maybe also make the needed telephone call you handed to a convenience store clerk in chapter twelve?

Often the manipulation of plot to accomplish such telescoping of roles is far simpler than you might think. It simplifies your storytelling. And the side advantage you sometimes encounter is that the doorman—now slated to be onstage in nine chapters—can be developed into an interesting character in his own right, vastly enriching your novel!

Pleasant surprises abound for the novelist who looks for new and unanticipated ways to make more and better use of existing plot developments *or* characters. Try it.

35

Don't Stop Too Soon

WRITING A STORY—ANY STORY—CAN BE A FATIGUING PROCESS. IF YOUR PROJECT has been a complex short story or—harder—a novel, you will probably come to the end of your first or second draft in a state not only of weariness, but also of a certain amount of anxiety. You want to be *done* with this arduous task—to have it finished and sent out somewhere, so you can at least relax a bit . . . and perhaps begin to think of some new project.

At such a time, when your enthusiasm for your current story is perhaps at an all-time low, and you ache both literally and figuratively, you run the grave risk of stopping a bit too soon—of failing to take one more critical look at what you planned to do, what you've ended up doing, and how well the job was done.

Good stories result from the writer's taking a few days off to rest, then returning to the fray to take one more cautious and caring look at the "finished" work.

Revise, revise and be ready to revise again. After all the work you've done, it would be tragic, wouldn't it, if you stopped a day or a month away from making those final adjustments which could make all the difference in the product's acceptability?

Now, it is possible to revise *too* often, too long. There are a few writers out there, I'm sure, who have worked and reworked the same dog-eared pages for many years or even decades when they would be far better off to let the story go, and get on with a new project on which they can use all they have learned. A part of wisdom is knowing when to let go like this, when to move ahead to the new.

A far more common error, however, lies in quitting just one read-through . . . one small set of changes . . . short of the ultimate goal: the best work you can do. You must beware the temptation to stop short just because you're tired and even discouraged. You must not stop on a project too soon.

What do you do if you decide to go through your present "finished" manuscript yet another time? No revision checklist can suggest everything you might look at. Your own awareness of your personal strengths and weaknesses as a writer, together with some idea of the kind of writer you want to become, will dictate some of the things high on your own checklist. What follows, however, is a suggestive list you might consider using as a basis for your own expanded one—things to do, questions to consider, things to check. Many of the questions assume you are to revise a novel-length manuscript, but most are equally applicable to a shorter tale.

1. *Give yourself a brief break.* After finishing—you think—the story, it's imperative that you give yourself a few days off away from it so you can rest a bit and allow your mind to clear. It may be months or years before you could hope to read your own story truly "cold," as if it were someone else's work, with any genuine objectivity. But even a week or two away from the project can provide you with some artistic distance, some perspective.

In the time off, you should not look at the manuscript. You should try not even to think much about it. *Pretend* it's out of your hair once and for all. Take a short trip, go to a party, read a couple of books, maybe even do some preliminary planning on another fiction project. The idea here is to separate yourself from the thing yet to be revised one more time. Then—

2. *Check the story for general acceptability.* Is there a length requirement or limit you must stay within? Have you followed guidelines or tipsheets, if available? Look back at your story plans? Does the finished story match up with the plan? (If you discover in the tipsheet that the heroine must be under thirty-five, for example, and somehow you made her forty-seven in your story, some obvious changes have to be made.)

3. *Read the manuscript straight through.* If possible, read it away from your work desk and even out of your office room. Except for a red pencil to mark typographical errors, don't plan to write notes during this reading. A tape recorder nearby is okay. But you are to try to make this a *reading experience*, not a writing or editing one. If you note problems, dictate notes on how to fix them, or merely dictate a note that the problem exists.

4. *Repair any problems found on the read-through.* This will involve going back to the word processor and writing or revising some pages. It's important to produce these now, in order, and get all your substitute pages neatly into the manuscript so it once again is "finished."

5. *Reexamine the opening of the story.* Is it gripping? Does it start with something happening—something that threatens the viewpoint character and sets her in motion toward some goal? Are you sure you didn't warm up your motors or describe a sunset to open?

6. *Study the viewpoint character(s).* One viewpoint must clearly dominate. Make sure of this. Count pages in each viewpoint if you must. Now look at ways you established the placement of the viewpoint. Is it clear where the viewpoint is at all times? Can you find any author intrusions that ought to be taken out? Any excursions into other viewpoints that are slips, or author self-indulgence rather than being required by the plot?

7. *Check the time scheme.* Make a chart if you have to, but make sure your timing is correct. Sometimes you can get this far and have two Tuesdays

in the same week, for example, or someone in Houston at noon and in New York an hour later. Make sure you have enough time pointers in the story so the reader always understands what time it is, what day it is, how this segment fits into the larger time scheme of the tale.

8. *Reexamine the character motivations.* At key points, is it perfectly clear what the story people want, and why? Just as important, at key points of stress in the story, have you made it clear to the reader why the character is hanging in there? Ask yourself: "Why doesn't my hero just resign from the plot and go home, here? Why must he carry on?"

9. *Look for coincidence.* Coincidence, as explained earlier, is nearly always bad, bad, bad. Make a conscious search for coincidence, especially of the kind that helps the viewpoint character. If you find a coincidence, figure out a way to fix it so the character has the desired experience by trying, rather than by luck.

10. *Read the chapter or section endings.* These are the spots where you most risk losing your reader. Do most of your sections or chapters end with developments that hook the reader with a new twist, disaster or realization that positively defies the reader to quit at that point? Of course they should.

11. *Think about total story logic.* Unless you're writing about crazy people, they'll all be trying to do things for what they see as good reasons, and they'll be trying to do things that will achieve their ends. Make sure you don't have any characters—especially the antagonist—doing things just because you the author wanted them to do that.

12 *Examine the ending.* The start of the story raised a problem, a character goal, and a story question. The ending must answer the question you posed at the outset. Does it? Clearly and unequivocally?

You may come up with many other checklist questions. These are enough to suggest the kind of process involved. As you can see, even this short list will force you to go back into the manuscript several times, looking for a specific possible problem—and none other—on each excursion. By isolating various possible problems in this way, you will see them more clearly if they exist.

Having done all these things (and probably others, too), you will at long last again have a finished manuscript, fixes in place, pages in order, everything ready to go.

By this time, too, you will probably hardly be able to bear looking at the stacked pages again.

That probably means you're really finished now . . . really ready to pronounce the story all done.

36

Don't Prejudice Your Editor

IT STANDS TO REASON THAT YOU WANT TO GET YOUR EDITOR TO READ YOUR story. Therefore, it's obvious that you want to present her with as attractive a package as possible. How do you accomplish this? By following standard literary manuscript form.

Put your story in the proper manuscript form, and you won't prejudice the editor at the outset.

Entire books have been written on manuscript form. You probably know as much about the subject as I do. However, just to be sure you don't make a ghastly mistake when you send something off, here are a few general observations.

1. *Everything must be typed.* The word "typed" also includes computer printouts *assuming the print is letter quality*. Many older nine-pin dot matrix printers will not fill the bill. If you can see dots in the letters, it isn't good enough. If the print is anything but bold and black and clean, it isn't good enough.

2. *Use good quality white paper*—at least 14-pound weight. Don't go beyond 20-pound weight; it's too thick and heavy. It doesn't have to be expensive bond. Editors these days are pretty used to getting manuscripts on photocopy machine-type paper, which usually works best with laser printers. Onion skin and coarse papers, however, remain unacceptable.

3. *Type on one side only, double-spaced.* This means *normal* double-spacing. Some machines put "double-spaced lines" almost on top of each other, and others put a vertical space in there that you could drive a truck through. Just because your printer calls it double-space doesn't necessarily mean it fits the standard set long ago on old manual and electronic machines. "Vacation portable double-space" is always too narrow. (And by the way, for heaven's sake don't stick extra spaces in between paragraphs, which drives editors nuts.)

4. *Use a standard typeface.* Pica or similar size. No funny typefaces.

5. *Use standard margins.* That means margins of one inch top, right and bottom, and inch and a half on the left. You may narrow the left margin a shade and increase the others a hair or two. Don't deviate widely from the

norm because (on the practical side) editors estimate words from standard page dimensions, and (on the emotional side) editors get mad when somebody sends them something that doesn't fit the accepted norm. (Most editors say they want ragged-right margins, not printer-justified ones. I think this is damned picky, but the editors say it is harder to estimate the size of the finished book if the manuscript is justified on the right.)

6. *Put your name and address on the first page*, near the top left if it's a short story and your copy is to be titled halfway down, and the story starts two-thirds of the way down. With a novel, a cover sheet with the title and your name and address is standard practice.

7. *Put your last name and a sequential page number top right on every page.* Some people use a word of the title rather than author name. I don't know why; the author name seems simpler. Number the pages *straight through*, beginning to end. Do *not* start each chapter with another page one, for example.

8. *At the end of the story, write The End.* Otherwise the editor might (no matter how wonderful your ending) start looking for another page. That's always bad. Give her a break; tell her when it's over.

Manuscripts of fewer than a dozen pages may be tri-folded and mailed in a regular envelope, if you insist. I personally think *all* manuscripts should be mailed flat, paper clipped (not stapled, glued or nailed) if a few pages, otherwise loose in a manuscript (stationery) box.

Covering letter? Sure, but keep it very brief. If you have some special expertise that makes you extraordinarily qualified to write this story, mention it. Otherwise just say in essence, "Here it is, hope you like it, I've enclosed an SASE (or postage) in case you don't."

If you're trying to hit a major market, it's a good idea to *query first*. A brief letter, saying who you are and what you want to submit, will suffice. Not only might this open the editor's door a tiny crack later, but no response to your query means "no"—which could save months when your unsolicited manuscript otherwise might languish on the floor beside the editor's desk with all the other unsolicited material.

Second, always keep a complete copy. If you're on a computer, duplicate your disks and keep a backup set somewhere else: your workday job office, if you have such a salaried job, in a bank box, or at a friend's home. Never assume a hard disk won't crash . . . or that the house or office might not burn down. Better to be redundant than sorry.

And finally, how long will an editor take to respond to your carefully prepared manuscript? Far too long, in most cases. Sad to say, you probably shouldn't even begin to worry until three or four months have passed. After that, a polite letter of inquiry might be in order. But do keep it polite. Editors may be rude, but they expect writers to be not only polite, but downright obsequious. If you write an angry letter after four months, demanding an *immediate* decision, or else(!), the letter may arrive just on the day the manuscript came back from its third outside reading with a "maybe" vote on acceptance for publication; now the editor is trying to decide whether to buy it or not. Guess what's going to happen if you prejudice her at that point!

37

Don't Give Up

"GIVING UP" COMES IN MANY FORMS. IF YOU ARE TO HAVE A GOOD CAREER AS A professional writer of fiction, you have to beware of all of them.

Here are some of the ways people give up, and so end up failures:

- They always put off new work, fearing new rejection.
- They always seem to be "just too busy today."
- They wait for inspiration.
- They claim they have too many distractions.
- They get discouraged, lose confidence, and let fear block them.
- They get angry and decide a cruel world is against them.
- They imagine a conspiracy against them and their kind of work.
- They blame fickle (or egregious) public taste.
- They come to believe new writers don't have a chance anymore.
- They say they always have bad luck.
- They use up all their creative energy in complaining.
-

I left an extra space so you can add one additional form of giving up that you may have observed in someone around you.

Of all the kinds listed, it seems to me that one of the most insidious is the last on my list: complaining. Did it ever occur to you that it takes just as much emotional and creative energy to complain as it does to write a few creative pages? It's true. Complaining and excuse-making represents negative energy, but it's energy nevertheless. Would-be fictioneers who spend a lot of time whining about their plight are boiling off creative calories that might be better invested in the positive task of writing a new story. In addition, complaining creates a negative attitude that tends to feed on itself. Optimists—doers—have a chance. Pessimists—who do nothing—spend all their time defining the nature of their failure, sometimes even before it takes place.

Regardless of how hard your struggle as a fiction writer may become, as long as you are studying, writing, and improving, you remain "in the hunt." The prize you seek may yet be yours. Your quest cannot be lost unless *you* choose to throw in the white towel.

If you find yourself getting stale or blocked or bitter, then, perhaps it would be well for you to recite some of the following litany. (One writer I know actually has some of these printed on 3×5 cards, and carries the cards with her so she can look at them several times a day.)

YOU *CAN* SELL WITHOUT AN AGENT.
PUBLISHERS *ARE* LOOKING FOR NEW WRITERS.
BEGINNERS *DO* BREAK IN EVERY YEAR.
YOU *DO NOT* HAVE TO LIVE IN NEW YORK TO SUCCEED.
YOUR NEXT STORY *WILL* BE BETTER.
YOUR LUCK IS *NOT* WORSE THAN MOST.
PERSISTENCE *WILL* WIN OUT.
THE STRUGGLE *IS* WORTH MAKING.
YOU *DO* HAVE ENOUGH TALENT.
ANYTHING YOU STILL NEED TO KNOW *CAN* BE LEARNED.
TOMORROW *WILL* LOOK BRIGHTER.

As a developing talent, every famous writer in the world today went through dark times when he or she had to recite truths like this and fight to maintain faith in them. Popular myth to the contrary, there are no "overnight successes" among good writers. Each and every one of them went through a long and arduous apprenticeship, and most of them probably suffered periods of doubt and even despair every bit as bad as any you might have. You must not slip into the habit of complaining or making other excuses. To do so is to give up, and among successful people that isn't an option, simply isn't allowed.

Finally, one more note about not giving up. When you have finished a manuscript and sent it off to a publisher, it may very well come back. It's not unusual for a story to be rejected a number of times, then find a home. I wrote a novel once that my agent sent to every fiction publisher we could think of, and all of them turned it down. A year or two later, *a new publisher* started business, and my agent sent it to an editor there. That new house bought it, and it was reasonably successful when published. I know of at least one best-seller that was rejected *seventeen times* before being accepted. It then sold a hundred thousand copies in hard covers.

Knowing all this, you must also guard against giving up too soon on any given manuscript. If and when it comes back, you must turn it around and send it out to someone else. If and when it comes back that time, you must have the persistence to send it out again. The process may take months or, in the case of book-lengths, even years. You must persist. Until the manuscript has been rejected six to eight times, it hasn't even been tried yet!

Will you get discouraged? Oh my yes. Will you want to put the manuscript in the closet to save yourself additional postage and potential disappointment? Of course. Will you have self-doubts? Naturally. Will you refuse to give up—and send it out still again? Yes!

Thus you will persist with the submission of finished projects and continue to fight disappointment that might stop your future work. In the course of this ongoing effort, you may doggedly write more stories of the same kind, intent on perfecting yourself with this kind of tale. Or you may try a different kind of fiction—a different length, different genre, different style. Either approach is fine. Neither is a sign of giving up. A willingness to strive for improvement through experimentation is just one hallmark of a writer still in the fight, refusing to give up. And so is a continued effort in the same vein.

If you refuse to give up, and press on regardless of discouraging events, you will find after a while that the ongoing effort in itself gives you new strength and hope. I don't understand exactly why this is so, but it is. The only way you can really ruin yourself is by giving up—under any of the guises that such a surrender may take.

Keep going. Ultimately, nothing else matters.

38

Don't Just Sit There

SO WE COME TO THE END OF THIS BOOK. THE LAST PAGES HERE, HOWEVER, should mean a beginning for you, wherever you may be.

Maybe you have nothing completed right now, but have an idea for a story . . . or a partial manuscript. If so, the end of this book signals the time you should get back to work on your project, and without delay.

But perhaps you already have a fiction project finished and submitted somewhere . . . in the mail.

If the latter, please note that one of two things can happen to it: It can either be rejected or it can be bought. If it's rejected, you need to have another project in the works so the momentary pain of the rejection will be diluted by your faith and hope in the later project. If it's bought, you need to have another project under way so you can send it out, too, and *soon*, and possibly sell it as well.

Whatever your circumstances, as a writer of fiction you need to be continually involved in the writing process. As noted at the very beginning of this brief excursion through some of the "don'ts," being at work makes future work seem easier, better oiled. For the sake of keeping your imagination smooth and your work habits disciplined, you must make a continuous effort.

Also, please note this: no writer can count on making a career out of one story or even one book. (Even Margaret Mitchell had written a tremendous amount of fiction, much unpublished, before her classic *Gone With the Wind*. And there is reason to believe that if she had lived, she would have written and published again.)

Your writing career, in other words, cannot be a one-shot operation. No matter how successful your last-completed story may become, you are going to need to write again.

Which is still another reason why you simply can't afford to sit around, waiting to see what happens to the last story . . . waiting for inspiration . . .

waiting for *anything*. Whatever happens tomorrow, you need to be writing when it does.

So continue your current project now, today. Or start a new one. Now. Today. Don't sit around another moment.

Luck!

Index

A

B

C

D

N

O

P

Q

R

S

T

V

W

Other Books of Interest

Annual Market Books

Children's Writer's & Illustrator's Market, edited by Lisa Carpenter (paper) $16.95
Guide to Literary Agents & Art/Photo Reps, edited by Robin Gee $15.95
Novel & Short Story Writer's Market, edited by Robin Gee (paper) $18.95
Writer's Market, edited by Mark Kissling $25.95

General Writing Books

Discovering the Writer Within, by Bruce Ballenger & Barry Lane $17.95
How to Write a Book Proposal, by Michael Larsen $10.95
Make Your Words Work, by Gary Provost $17.95
Pinckert's Practical Grammar, by Robert C. Pinckert (paper) $11.95
The 29 Most Common Writing Mistakes & How To Avoid Them, by Judy Delton (paper) $9.95
The Writer's Book of Checklists, by Scott Edelstein $16.95
The Writer's Digest Guide to Manuscript Formats, by Buchman & Groves $18.95
The Writer's Essential Desk Reference, edited by Glenda Neff $19.95

Fiction Writing

Characters & Viewpoint, by Orson Scott Card $13.95
The Complete Guide to Writing Fiction, by Barnaby Conrad $17.95
Cosmic Critiques: How & Why 10 Science Fiction Stories Work, edited by Asimov & Greenberg (paper) $12.95
Creating Characters: How To Build Story People, by Dwight V. Swain $16.95
Dialogue, by Lewis Turco $13.95
The Fiction Writer's Silent Partner, by Martin Roth $19.95
Handbook of Short Story Writing: Vol 1, by Dickson and Smythe (paper) $10.95
Handbook of Short Story Writing: Vol. II, edited by Jean Fredette (paper) $12.95
Manuscript Submission, by Scott Edelstein $13.95
Mastering Fiction Writing, by Kit Reed $18.95
Plot, by Ansen Dibell $13.95
Theme & Strategy, by Ronald B. Tobias $13.95

Special Interest Writing Books

Armed & Dangerous: A Writer's Guide to Weapons, by Michael Newton (paper) $14.95
Deadly Doses: A Writer's Guide to Poisons, by Serita Deborah Stevens with Anne Klarner (paper) $16.95
Hillary Waugh's Guide to Mysteries & Mystery Writing, by Hillary Waugh $19.95
How to Pitch & Sell Your TV Script, by David Silver $17.95
How to Write & Sell True Crime, by Gary Provost $17.95
How to Write Mysteries, by Shannon OCork $13.95
How to Write Romances, by Phyllis Taylor Pianka $13.95
How to Write Science Fiction & Fantasy, Orson Scott Card $13.95
How to Write Tales of Horror, Fantasy & Science Fiction, edited by J.N. Williamson (paper) $12.95
Successful Scriptwriting, by Jurgen Wolff & Kerry Cox (paper) $14.95
The Writer's Complete Crime Reference Book, by Martin Roth $19.95

The Writing Business

The Complete Guide to Self-Publishing, by Tom & Marilyn Ross (paper) $16.95
A Writer's Guide to Contract Negotiations, by Richard Balkin (paper) $11.95
The Writer's Guide to Self-Promotion & Publicity, by Elane Feldman $16.95
Writing A to Z, edited by Kirk Polking $22.95

To order directly from the publisher, include $3.00 postage and handling for 1 book and $1.00 for each additional book. Allow 30 days for delivery.

Writer's Digest Books, 1507 Dana Avenue, Cincinnati, Ohio 45207
Credit card orders call TOLL-FREE
1-800-289-0963

Prices subject to change without notice.

Write to this same address for information on *Writer's Digest* magazine, *Story* magazine, Writer's Digest Book Club, Writer's Digest School, and Writer's Digest Criticism Service.